The Book Shopper

The Book Shopper

A Life in Review

MURRAY BROWNE

Paul Dry Books

Philadelphia   2009

First Paul Dry Books Edition, 2009

Paul Dry Books, Inc.
Philadelphia, Pennsylvania
www.pauldrybooks.com

Text type: Berkeley Oldstyle
Display type: Post Mediaeval Italic
Designed & composed by P. M. Gordon Associates
Author photo: Sean Casey

1 3 5 7 9 8 6 4 2
Printed in the United States of America

Library of Congress Cataloging-in-Publication Data

Browne, Murray.
  The book shopper : a life in review / Murray Browne. —
1st Paul Dry Books ed.
      p.   cm.
ISBN 978-1-58988-056-6 (alk. paper)
  1. Browne, Murray—Books and reading. 2. Books and reading—
United States. I. Title.
  Z1003.2B76 2009
  028'.9 0973—dc22

                                                        2009002700

For Bonnie, Cynthia, Denise,
and my mother, Jean

Contents

PART ONE

The Principles of Book Shopping

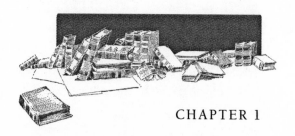

CHAPTER 1

About the Author: An Introductory Memoir

LIKE THE SCOTTISH WRITER Alasdair Gray, who refers to himself in *A History Maker* (1996) as a "fat, old asthmatic Glaswegian who lives by painting and writing," I'm naturally inclined to resort to self-deprecation when I describe myself. Although conventional marketing dogma says I should showcase my credentials and achievements, bragging about my triumphs is in direct conflict with the twin pillars of Midwestern virtue I grew up with: pathological humility and excessive modesty. Besides, on the surface my life looks somewhat underwhelming.

I grew up in Milford, Illinois, the Buckle on the Corn Belt, a place where life revolved around farming, drinking, and attending church. Not such a dull place to grow up, really. For the youth, there were the temptations of finding out what Dad's Plymouth could do on those treeless highway slabs between the cornfields. For adults, there was the potential danger of farm machinery—horrible accidents involving grain augers or tractors flipping on their sides. In town, you'd see the survivors, like Civil War amputees, limping into Elmer's Barber Shop (no appt. needed) or chugging up to the drive-through window at the Corner Tap (open on Sunday, just like church), ordering a gin 'n' tonic in a plastic cup to go.

I lived in the country, but I wasn't a farm kid. My father was an accountant at the local canning factory. My grandmother told me that Dad was a big reader as a kid, but when I knew him his book tastes didn't range far from the Ballantine War series, and it seemed that a copy of *Hitler Moves East: 1941– 1943* (1965) was always on top of the toilet tank.* My mother's favorite book was *Gone with the Wind*, which she once gave me for my birthday. It didn't take me but a few pages to realize that this was the Number One Girls Book of All Time (the male characters are imbeciles, totally preoccupied with fighting that "silly war" rather than paying attention to Scarlett), and further reading explained why many of the seventh- and eighth-grade girls had hugged copies of the Margaret Mitchell novel to their budding bosoms.

* My father's *Hitler Moves East* should not be confused with *Hitler Moves East: A Graphic Chronicle, 1941–43* (1977) with photographs by David Levinthal and text by Garry Trudeau (of *Doonesbury* fame), which was recently reissued.

I give the North American publication date (or copyright date when I didn't have a copy of a book with me) because book shopping is an activity that spans a lifetime of searching for and re-evaluating older books, and I wanted to give a sense of their longevity. In general, I give a date the first time a book is mentioned in a chapter. Dates for old-timey classics and book series are not included.

Unlike the farm kids who were kept busy in the fields, I didn't grow up spending endless hours on a John Deere, and I was often alone. My mother would say I was "good at entertaining myself" as I played army in the run-off ditches that bordered our house or created entire seasons of action with my football cards on the rec room rug. In school, I seemed more of a nonparticipating observer. Culturally, my options in rural Illinois were limited to piano lessons from an organ salesman with tobacco-stained hands or church sermons. As an athlete, I managed to set school records for bench warming (no small feat considering our meager enrollments). I suppose this set the stage for my becoming a full-fledged "exile in residence," a label I adopted for myself as a person who on the surface looks and acts normal (like your neighbor), but underneath is a corn-fed, Dylan-listening anarchist. Still, I was a likable fellow and entertained my classmates with humor. My humor was not the class clown variety but a more sophisticated brand of stuff, like a spoof on our school newspaper, the product of an education that included poring over issues of *Mad* magazine.

I attended Indiana University, graduating with a degree in English and in Radio and Television. I couldn't say whether Indiana had a great English Department or not, but I was introduced to dozens of writers who appealed to my sense of irreverence. I also met my future ex-wife, and for the next twenty years I followed her circuitous career path, which took us to relatively uneventful places such as Champaign, Illinois, Wichita, Kansas (where our older daughter was born), West Lafayette, Indiana (where our second daughter was born), Holland, Michigan (opted for a good shepherd-husky this time), and finally to Oak Ridge, Tennessee. In Tennessee, I realized that my set of marital problems had become like those unopened boxes of dishes or old toys that grow too large and heavy to carry any more. Moving regularly for another person's career blocked the path to my own career. But I'm not whining here. First of all, I spent a lot of quantity, as opposed to quality, time with my daughters. Second, important jobs are time consuming. My succession of dead-end jobs, such as night operator at a classical music station or at the university computing center, gave me more time to read, think, and write than I would have had in most occupations. Also during these long days at home with the children, there was some time to read during their naps or when I took them to the pool. I was hardly a micromanager or a perfectionist when it came to housekeeping. As a result, both daughters learned to do their own hair at very early ages.

No matter where I lived or was employed, I found that books grew in their ability to connect me to something, a link to other cultures and ideas. It was comforting to know that I could "talk books." Even if I didn't have a PhD or live in an upscale neighborhood, I gleaned bits and pieces from enough books to hold a conversation with the most insatiable readers, no matter what their social or economic position. Moreover, books are relatively cheap entertainment. Over the years, I expanded my pleasure without busting my budget by browsing used bookstores instead of the full-priced chains.

This predilection has grown into a real (albeit quirky) passion for thinking about the many ways books affect our lives—how and where we shop for them, the people we know who read them, the small passages that stick in our heads for years only to reappear at the oddest moments. The minds of book people are mosaics of ideas, thoughts, and phrases that have originated in books. In her collection of book-related essays, *Ex Libris: Confessions of a Common Reader* (1998), Anne Fadiman writes that the heart of reading is "not whether we wish to purchase a new book but how we maintain our connections with our old books." I'm fascinated by how we hold and shape these fragments, how they coalesce into what I call my book shopper state of mind.

My book shopper state of mind is not to be confused with that of the über book shopper, the book collector, or the bibliophile. You may recognize these types. The über shopper is the person who simply likes to shop for bargains on anything just to "save money." Actually reading the book is irrelevant. This shopper cannot resist the lure of getting down on hands and knees to go through boxes of books at garage sales or queuing up early to beat the rush at the annual library book sale or spending the whole afternoon at an abandoned supermarket that has reopened (for about a month) as a book warehouse. All this just to brag about getting a grocery sack full of books for a dollar.

Then there is the book collector, who relishes autographed first editions of contemporary writers or seventeenth-century rarities that look ready to crumble at the touch of a hand. These collectors don't necessarily engage the written word either, especially if they like to eat while reading. A funnel cake can wreak hell on a James Joyce first edition. Besides, book collecting is an expensive hobby. The third type of book shopper is the bibliophile—those book-reading junkies who shoot through a book a day. Their reading habits are noble, but I wouldn't want to use their bathroom.

Admittedly, I am part über shopper, part book collector, and part bibliophile, but I am basically a person who obsesses on moderation. I was an über shopper until I realized that I was buying more books than I would ever read in my lifetime. Now, I restrain myself from making a beeline to every used bookstore I discover. While walking along the street, I avoid making eye contact with even the most pathetic table of cheap hardbacks whose tattered covers hide their broken book lives. Still, I do have my impulsive moments and the credit card bills to prove it.

As far as being a collector, there are certain authors I like well enough to collect hardback versions of their work, because in general, hardcovers are more durable and resistant to yellowing than paperbacks. If I had the money, I'd drop a couple hundred dollars on a hardback copy of *V.* (1963) just to round out my Thomas Pynchon collection, but I haven't done so—yet.

Nowadays, I am a lame excuse for a bibliophile because my annual goal has slipped to reading twenty good books a year, which may seem to be a surprisingly low figure to some of you. I wish I had more time, but I have other commitments (work, family, writing, cleaning). Besides, as you'll see in the next chapter, I have some childhood issues concerning reading lists.

I suspect that I will continue to reside in the intersection of all these types of shoppers. It allows me to share a bond with the three basic types of book people, while not being sucked into just one way of looking at our relationships with books. It is my belief that all active readers have this mélange of book shoppers in them, and thus my own experiences may resonate with yours. I invite you to accompany me, "a real-life character," as we troll through the backwaters of contemporary books and book culture far away from the mainstream madness of bestsellers, literary criticism (the term "fin-de-siècle" is only used once), and book megastores. Along the way, I'll introduce you to a few books and authors you might be interested in pursuing on your own. Most of the books I refer to are not a challenge to find. You can buy them at any reputable used bookstore, or if you prefer to forgo the book-hunting

Early Influences

Perhaps all readers and writers can look back and point to the person who introduced them to the power—or as we humbly downplay it in the Midwest, the utility—of words. For me, it was my paternal grandmother, who lived only ten miles from us. She graduated with a degree in journalism from the University of Illinois after World War I (no small accomplishment for a woman in those days) and taught in a one-room schoolhouse, which she later purchased. Our family would have Halloween bonfires at the schoolhouse in the fall.

Ironically, she didn't own many books, preferring to borrow from the local library, where she served on the board. She always had a small stack of books next to her favorite reading chair, which was one of those motorized, vibrating chaise lounge monsters. She purchased the ten volumes of *My Book House* for our family, though it was my mother who actually read the stories and poems to us. Later, she bought me a copy of *Bartlett's Quotations*.

I think what impressed me most about my grandmother was her ability to quote lines of poetry

experience I still crave, they can be purchased readily online or ordered from your favorite bookstore. The last chapters of the book look at what you do with these books once you have them. What is their real value?

with great ease. I had heard from my father that she could recite *The Rubáiyát of Omar Khayyám* by heart. She didn't live a particularly eventful life, since dealing with my grandfather was excitement enough. She described the experience as "Nobody knows the trouble I've seen—except Gellhorn" (a reference to Ernest Hemingway's third wife). She showed me that a person who did a lot of reading was naturally interesting.

In college I started reading the *New York Times Book Review*, and rather than let me toss them out, my grandmother asked me to save them for her. Later she stored the copies in her schoolhouse. After her death, arsonists torched the place. The *Book Reviews* provided the tinder, no doubt, much like the kindling she provided for my lifelong interest in words.

The chapters of this book are mostly informal essays interspersed with short "Bookmarks" related to a life with books. A word of advice on how to read this book comes from the antiwar journalist Raymond Mungo. In the introduction to his book *Famous Long Ago: My Life and Hard Times with Liberation News Service* (1970), Mungo insisted that his readers "take it slow, don't try to read it in one sitting, by all means get distracted from time to time. Read it stoned, read it straight, give up and never finish it, it's all the same between friends. Take care of your health and get plenty of rest."

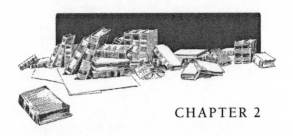

CHAPTER 2

How I Became a Reader

TODAY, SCHOOLS PROVIDE a healthy variety of activities ranging from sports to dance to technology clubs, but when I was growing up in a small farm town in Illinois in the late 1960s and attending Milford Elementary Grade School, opportunities for broadening one's horizons were almost non-existent. The school's only acknowledgment of culture beyond the town was a World War II buzz bomb that was perched on the lawn just a bottle's throw from a drive-up liquor store.

This explains the revered status of boys like Curt and Benny, who started on the Milford Bats eighth-grade basketball team. Basketball was the only activity outside the classroom in which a boy could distinguish himself. Playing on this team was worth the wind sprints and extra free throw practice just to have the pretty Milford Bats cheerleaders—pixies with green pleated velvet skirts and white knit sweaters—jumping up and down cheering for you.

Although my desire was deep, my athletic ability was shallow, and I spent most of the time on the bench. The coach did take advantage of my ability to handle statistics, and sometimes I would keep the books during a game, until the time I alerted the scorekeeper that one of our players had failed to check in properly. The coach yelled at me when our team was charged with a technical foul.

Starved for notoriety beyond the realm of sports, I looked for other venues of recognition and found the Class Reading List. Our eighth-grade teacher, Mrs. Smith, required each student to keep track of every book he or she read over the school year. Lists were kept in a folder in the classroom library, but a report or review of the book was not required. It was strictly an honor system. At this time I had already read several books on the Civil War and basketball. Most of the kids hadn't read any books at all except for Debbie, a quiet, heavy-set girl who attended the same church I did. You would always see her with a mystery or a book about nursing. At Sunday school, she could easily read aloud her Bible verses and wasn't intimidated by the rowdy Sunday school boys who dominated our classroom. Our class included the younger brother of the village psychopath, who once pushed me through the basement drywall during Youth Group.* Debbie didn't say much, but when

---

* I mention this because these two brothers were also known as avid readers. They'd blow off classes, get suspended from school, and get in fights on a regular basis, but when they weren't in trouble you could see them reading a book in study hall. They were probably our school's best readers, but they'd be goddamned before they would fill out some reading list.

she did, she'd roll her eyes and shake her head at our immaturity.

Somehow it dawned on me that I could be the king of readers. I would read books. Lots of books. More books than anyone else. More books even than Debbie, who at the midway point of the school year had already listed more than twenty titles. I would be to reading what Curt and Benny were to basketball. The competition would not be nearly so keen—just Debbie and me. And I wasn't even going to tell her.

In the months that followed, I became what's known as a voracious reader, buzzsawing through books about General Custer and the Supreme Court. Debbie was still ahead of me, but I was gaining.

You might think that my grades would have improved, but they did not. I became so obsessed with reading that I neglected my studies, including assignments in reading class. Even more surprising, I became a crummier reader. In an effort to read as many books as possible, I took shortcuts. I searched out short books (200 pages maximum) and learned that large print could increase my speed dramatically. (I thought I was so brilliant with these strategies.) Sad to report, I soon reached the point of skimming the first half of a book—one about Mary Queen of the Scots, say (my choice of books at the school library was becoming limited)—and convincing myself that the book was dumb and not worth finishing. Still, I added it to my list.

Using such methods I finally caught Debbie and passed her. Then I began to brag to my friends, parents, and the teacher about how much I was reading. I was surprised that Mrs. Smith did not catch on to my duplicitous behavior, especially after I scored below average on my eighth-grade reading exam. She still believed that I had read all those books from cover to cover. Perhaps she theorized that I was just a pathetic reader in the first place.

Up to this point the situation was a harmless and forgettable one, but an assembly at the end of the school year changed all that. Ironically, it was in the Home of the Bats, the gym with the flaky, mint green paint, the scene of some of my greatest disappointments, that I would be, for a moment, the center of attention.

At this final assembly, the entire seventh- and eighth-grade classes (almost 100 students!) sat in the bleachers that filled half of the gym. The coaches handed out basketball letters to the real athletes, and the music teacher handed out plastic pins, shaped like little lutes or eighth notes, to kids who participated in the band. I was uninterested in the whole affair until Mrs. Smith announced that they were going to give out special academic awards.

The first was for spelling, which went to Steve. Next, an award for mathematics, but I didn't even bother to raise my head, and Bobby quickly took the honors. Then Mrs. Smith announced that there would be an award for reading. I heard some of the kids whisper my name. And sure enough: "The 1969 Milford Elementary Grade School Award for Reading goes to Murray Browne." There was some polite clapping and mockery and I was embarrassed but not enough to keep me from going up there and claiming the hardware.

While at center court, I felt like someone who was accepting an award for someone else, like the person who accepts an Oscar for a dead or reluctant friend. Thank God they didn't ask me to say a few words about reading.

Sometimes in stories like this the narrator breaks down in guilt, confesses to his peers that he is unworthy of the award and hands it over to the real winner—which would have been Debbie, of course. But nothing like that happened. I successfully avoided her eyes, and exhilaration carried the day. I felt no guilt or remorse until I got home with my prize.

I set the trophy on a shelf in my bedroom and looked at it. It was a nice trophy, a golden statuette of a slim woman holding a wreath (representing scholarship, no less), standing on a marble stone base. I was excited at first, because the trophy girl looked like one of the Bat cheerleaders holding a pompom, and the base had my name engraved on it. But the more I looked at it, the worse I felt, and it came to pass (a biblical time reference) that I put the trophy away in my closet.

Though I don't read competitively anymore, I still do read quite a bit. Probably not as much as you might think for someone who has written a book called *The Book Shopper*, but definitely more than most people. Perhaps part of this can be attributed

Heroes in Blue and Gray

Published in 1965 as part of Whitman Publishing's
Real Life Stories series, Robert E. Alter's *Heroes in
Blue and Gray* was by far my favorite book as a kid.
Even before my dubious success as an award-win-
ning reader, I had read and reread the book so many
times that my parents took my brother and me on a
trip to Shiloh and Atlanta (and we weren't a family
that did vacations). Looking over my yellowed copy
now, I appreciate that Alter was a concise writer,
covering the four years of war in a taut 212 pages
(complete with graphic illustrations and maps).*
Alter was thorough in describing all the major bat-
tles, among them Shiloh, Antietam, Gettysburg, and
Chickamauga. For each battle, he focused on one
historical figure, such as Ulysses S. Grant at Shiloh
and Robert E. Lee at Chancellorsville. Even though
Alter admits in the fine print of the book that he
created imaginary conversations between the main
personalities, I have felt over the years that the
book is amazingly accurate in its encapsulation of

---

* Not as graphic, though, as the Topps Civil War trading cards
that my brother and I also collected during the mid-1960s. These
cards were deliciously gory, with plenty of bayonets, blood, and
evocative titles such as Death Battle, Painful Death, and Wave of
Death.

to the recognition I received on that awards day long
ago. Unfortunately, I know I can't ever give Debbie
the trophy she deserved, but I do want to thank her
for not calling me out during that assembly. I don't
credit her discretion to the lessons of forgiveness

each battle, though I am a little wary of his phonetic interpretation of the forever-lost Rebel yell (EEEE YU YU YUUuuu).

I experienced again the relish with which I read Alter when I read Shelby Foote's three-volume, nearly 3000-page, *The Civil War: A Narrative*. The first volume was published in 1958 and the last in 1974. I have plans for a passage from Foote's tome to be read at my funeral. This particular passage came to my attention while watching the final segment of Ken Burns's documentary, where Foote recites (with the longing, ethereal violins of "Ashokan Farewell" in the background) a soldier's eulogy to his comrades known as "Was It Not Real."*

The Alter book sparked my lifelong interest in the Civil War, which later translated into an appreciation of storytelling in all its forms, and that's something I'll take to the grave with me. How more full-circle can you get than that?

* Incidentally, this same film clip in the Ken Burns documentary has a short "sound bite" of the Rebel yell. You can hear it on You-Tube and judge for yourself.

taught in Sunday school; she probably discounted the incident because she already knew—years ahead of me—that serious reading has its own rewards far beyond some pathetic trophy.

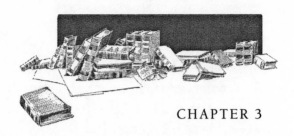

CHAPTER 3

A Reviewer's Lament

I USED TO REVIEW books for my local newspaper. After ten years, I "retired," but there was no celebratory dinner in my honor attended by happy authors (who received free publicity) or grateful readers who heeded my advice on which books should definitely be read and which shunned. I guess it should have come as no surprise, since local book reviewers rank on the literary scene somewhere between an Amazon.com customer-reviewer and an advertising copywriter for Books-a-Million.

I got my big break in the early 1990s when the *Grand Rapids Press* asked thousands of its Sunday readers if they'd like to try their skills at reviewing. The newspaper asked book lovers to tell what kind of books they liked, and the editor would select something for each one to review. Approximately one hundred of us replied to the call. (Only a hundred! Imagine if they had wanted TV or movie reviewers.) I told the editor that I liked a) contemporary literary fiction, b) offbeat fiction, and c) any nonfiction as long as it had something to do with baseball. No mysteries, no westerns, no sci-fi, and no bestsellers, please! My debut review (you always remember the first) was Nadine Gordimer's *My Son's Story* (1990). I summarized the Nobel Prize winner's novel about the clay feet of a South African rights activist in less than 150 words, which apparently pleased the editor because she continued to send me books to review. The newspaper even paid me.

The second book I reviewed was a strange offering titled *Something Leather* (1991), from the obscure Scottish writer and illustrator Alasdair Gray. Although I did not know this at the time, Gray is about as wacky an artist as you'll find. *Something Leather*, the story of an unhappy woman who shops for clothes at a strange back alley boutique, and of the shop's owner, who takes it upon herself to awaken the woman's sensibilities, is Gray's most approachable book. This was just the beginning of my plunge into the backwaters of contemporary literature. I'd take on weird novels like the one that had a teeny-tiny worm boy who lived inside another character's head. Then there was the one in which the protagonist eats a skunk to survive in post-apocalyptic America. (How does this goofy stuff ever get published?) Periodically these kinds of books would arrive at my doorstep, and I would review them in a timely fashion without complaint. Occasionally I would talk to the editor on the phone, but I never met her in person. It's unusual to have someone whom you've never met pick books for you to read—but then again, that's what reviewers do for their readers.

Reviewing had its pleasures and its drawbacks. It introduced me to some good writers such as Gray and Roy Lewis,* but then I'd get books that were torture to read. I read every book I was assigned, but admittedly my reading rate sped up considerably if the book was awful. Over a period of time, I established a few rules. If the writer was a first-time author, I would cut him or her some slack. I aspired to be a first-time author myself someday and hoped to receive the same courtesy. The only exception I made was *The Search for Savin' Sam* (1998), by first-time author William Carter, who was former President Jimmy Carter's nephew and son of Billy "Beer" Carter. It was obvious that the book was published and marketed based solely on the writer's lineage, and the publisher's claim that Carter was "a new Southern voice" was completely bogus. I was so incensed at the entire sham that at the end of my review I wrote "the only way *The Search for Savin' Sam* could be worthy of being called Southern literature is if the book received the Flannery O'Connor misfit treatment. It needs to be taken out to the woods and shot."

I subjected established and experienced writers to higher standards and more barbarous comments, even though I doubted my views affected anyone's career. In ten years of reviewing, I received feedback only once: an email from a reader who claimed

---

* Roy Lewis wrote *The Evolution Man*. See Chapter 10, "Humorists: Being Funny Can Be Such a Chore."

that I could not have read Wendell Berry's lengthy novel about a small town barber, *Jayber Crow* (2001), because if I had, I would never have referred to it as "a tome of below-average fiction."

I found it easiest to write reviews for books I absolutely loathed. After reading a lengthy book with a hackneyed plot, such as one of Larry McMurtry's sequels to *Lonesome Dove* (1985), I was fairly lathered up for having been subjected to such dreck, and the vitriol flowed effortlessly.* It was as easy as writing a complaint letter to the catalog company that sells you the "wrinkle-magnet" dress shirts. Conversely, the most difficult book review was the one where I liked the book tremendously and envied its craftsmanship. How do you express your undying admiration for a Jim Harrison book without sounding syrupy or falling back on the "masterpiece" cliché?

Left in between were the lesser books with a few redeeming qualities and the decent books with a serious flaw or two. These average books are the majority of the ones for review, and over the years, this contributed to my formulaic approach to review writing. I'd begin with something I perceived as witty or pithy in the lead paragraph, followed by a description of the book's plot and main characters. Then, depending on its type of averageness, I'd point out the book's strengths or weaknesses and wrap up with

---

* This is difficult to say, McMurtry being the patron saint of book shoppers. See Chapter 11.

something pithy or witty that tied back to the lead. The final line was supposed to leave my readers with an indelible impression about me as a reviewer-with-style. (Their impression of the book was secondary.) During this time, I learned to keep my prose tight, because the book editor at the *Knoxville News-Sentinel* (the second paper where I reviewed) was exacting in her editing practices and followed the dictum that any words that hogged too much space were to be deleted unceremoniously. The meaning of words did not factor in her decision to cut them. It didn't take me long to realize that unless I wanted my reviews to read like book jacket blurbs (without ellipses no less . . .) I'd better learn to keep within the 300 to 500 word limit.

Further aggravating my situation at the *Knoxville News-Sentinel* was the fact that they refused to pay for book reviews. At the time I moved from Grand Rapids, Michigan, to Knoxville, Tennessee, reviewing had given me some self-identity—a quality you do not want to surrender when you move to a new area of the country—so I agreed to review *gratis*. I hoped that reviewing at the paper would help me get my foot in the door for freelance feature writing. Eventually (though reviewing had little to do with it) the paper hired me as a stringer to cover the Oak Ridge City Council. That small city in eastern Tennessee was founded in 1942 specifically as the base of operations for the Manhattan Project and the making of the first atomic bomb. Oddly enough, covering Oak Ridge council meetings was like re-

Gray and Bell

I'm not the only one who admires Alasdair Gray. National Book Award finalist Madison Smartt Bell, in his acknowledgments for his novel *Doctor Sleep* (1991), recognized Gray as one of the people who contributed to his book. However, Bell quipped, Gray "will hardly be expecting it." For years after I read the acknowledgment, I wondered what it meant. At the Nashville Book Festival I saw Bell on a panel, but I was too shy to quiz him in front of a packed house. Still, it continued to bother me how these two seemingly disconnected writers were linked—Gray, an off-the-wall writer and illustrator from Scotland, and Bell, a novelist whose trilogy of books about the slave revolt in Haiti is an incredible work of history and imagination. (Beyond all the scholarship and national acclaim, Bell's *All Souls' Rising* [1995] is a real page-turner. The book follows the actions of three characters: one based on an historical figure, the rebellion's leader, François Dominique Toussaint-Louverture, and two purely fictional characters, Dr. Antoine Hébert, and the runaway slave, Riau. Each chapter is written

viewing a morality play as the city council members grappled with the decision of how to embrace the legacy of the Bomb and all its trimmings, including co-existing with the Oak Ridge National Laboratory and the Y-12 National Security Complex. Should they promote their historical roots with events such as a Secret City Festival and the banging of the Japas a stand-alone, almost serialized, episode, which lends a degree of suspense throughout the book.)

Finally I had an opportunity to hear Bell give another reading, this time at Maryville College in Maryville, Tennessee. A writer friend of mine was doing the handling of Bell and invited me to attend. After the reading, Bell graciously answered all the standard writing-student questions: Where do get your inspiration? What is your workday like? How do you get a goddamn agent? Since the discourse in the half-filled auditorium was lagging and I *did* really want to know, I decided to ask my question. Bell didn't miss a beat in answering that Gray's bawdy book *1982, Janine* (1984) had influenced him while he was writing *Doctor Sleep*. Bell and my friend were pleased enough by the odd question to invite me to join them for the post-lecture beer and literary chat. Thank you, Alasdair Gray—although I hardly think he will be expecting it.

anese-style peace gong or concentrate on building a new identity by bulldozing the "distressed shopping mall" (a term I learned as a reporter) and replacing it with quaint little shops?

In contrast to writing about books, I was paid for these city council theater reviews (and believe me there was a flair for drama at budget time), and I received many more comments in the supermarket checkout line than I ever had for my book opinions. The inequity in recognition, coupled with my lack of payment (even a pittance would have made a differ- ence), smacked of such unfairness. I'd spend seven or eight hours reading a book and maybe three or fours hours writing and polishing a review for nothing. In the meantime, the newspaper's movie and tele- vision reviewers were getting paid. It wasn't right! How long does it take to watch a movie? Besides, movie and TV reviewers were allowed to use the star system for evaluating the arts, with its little icons or bullets, or the "thumbs up" and "thumbs down" review. How tough is that?

As I look back now at my reviewing days, I wonder whether I acted a little hastily in retiring. Although I like to complain about the lack of money (or the respect—money and respect, that's how it is here in the West) and the mundane quality of my own writing, I still can't write the words "good rid- dance to reviewing" without a twinge of nostalgia. I tell myself that *The Book Shopper* is a type of book review experiment, and while that may be true, I do feel an element of uncertainty about what I'm put- ting on paper today. Will it ever be read by anyone else beyond a few close friends?

While reviewing, I never deluded myself that I was influencing readers, but I did believe that I was contributing something—minuscule as it was—to the world of books and words. The review page in the newspaper was a place of refuge in the towns of Grand Rapids and Knoxville, where books were important to a few people. I was part of that commu- nity, and those reviews were my citizenship papers.

Reviewing put me in the literary world, just not on the literary map. That explains the additional sense of uncertainty I've had with each change of address. Not only did I leave places and friends behind, but every time I moved to a new community I had to re-apply for those literary citizenship papers. And now, as I enter my second year of living in Atlanta, I wonder when (or if) I'll be granted another set of papers.

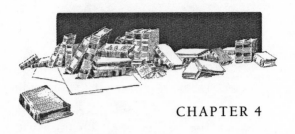

CHAPTER 4

Book Lovers Are Not Necessarily People Lovers

Books disturb people. They make them anti-social.
—Montag, in the movie *Fahrenheit 451*

I ONCE SHOPPED AT the British-American Used Bookstore in downtown Allegan, Michigan. It was a strange-looking store, located on the ground floor of a trapezoid-shaped building at the corner of a five-point intersection. A barbershop occupied the basement. Upon entering, I felt an extra jolt of anticipation at visiting a "British-American" bookstore— not your normal English language fanfare, I hoped. No salesperson greeted me, and as I looked around, I noticed what a miserable excuse for a used bookstore it was—heavy into romances, piles of yellowed *National Geographics*, high-school textbooks (circa 1950), all thrown on shelves or dumped in the aisles. The place reeked of cigarette smoke, and you could skate on the dusty wood floor. From the barbershop below, I could hear the soundtrack of an old *Perry Mason* show.

Before I could leave, the unkempt proprietor appeared, his wavy gray hair uncombed and the faint medicinal scent of Barbicide on his wrinkled clothes. He said he had been downstairs watching *Perry Mason*. As he lit a cigarette, he began to complain that Allegan was a stupid town, the capital of illiteracy in Michigan. I thought it better to say nothing, including a comment on the irony of his abandoning the store to watch TV—or of asking him who he thought was more debonair, Raymond Burr or Desi Arnaz.

He continued to rail and curse about life in the little town in southwestern Michigan. Not wanting to risk further irking this angry man or being thought a non-reader, I decided I'd better buy something. There was nothing remotely close to anything I liked, so I settled for a worn paperback of *Summer of '49* (1989) by David Halberstam, which was priced too high. I never went back to that bookstore and it closed soon afterward.

One time my friend Denise and I were browsing at a used bookstore near Vanderbilt University in Nashville. It met my collection standards, and it had the additional accouterments I like to find in used bookstores: a few antique glass-fronted bookcases, towers of shelves jammed with books stretching toward the high ceilings, indirect Tiffany lamp lighting, and a strong collection of Civil War books. But I didn't see my boyhood favorite, *Heroes in Blue and Gray*, and I wasn't about to ask if they had any Civil

War trading cards, because the man, who seemed to be the proprietor, was as crusty as that bookstore owner in Allegan. The place was littered with signs warning customers not to make noise or ask about photocopying. One rule scrawled on notebook paper suggested that parents control their kids by tethering them outside. Thankfully, there were no placards that prohibited loitering (which is a lot like browsing) or described stringent penalties for not wearing a shirt or shoes (no service) or defined the store's fiscal policies. ("We don't go to the bank asking for a Walker Percy book, so don't come here asking for change.") Denise purchased a twenty-dollar book about early Santa Fe architecture and he just grunted at her, once again proving my theory that used bookstore types are more inclined to keep to themselves than engage in bookish repartee.

These experiences illustrate one of the tenets of book shopping, namely, that book people are not necessarily people people. I realize many of us hold the preconception that people who love books—a phrase that always makes me cringe a little—are automatically warm and open to conversation. Based on my personal, anecdotal evidence, however, the opposite seems true. People working at used bookstores rarely look up from the book they are reading, whether to ask if you need assistance or even simply to recognize your presence. Since a landfill is usually more organized than the shelves of a used bookstore, you might well need help finding out whether Ian Frazier is buried in Fiction or Non-fiction, Humor or Travel. But providing a customer with some attention might lead to annoying conversation, so one is often greeted with a vacant look or sour acknowledgment.

I'm not the only one bold enough to verbalize the darker side of book people. In his book *Double Fold: Libraries and the Assault on Paper* (2001), Nicholson Baker explains the term "double fold," which comes from the practice of dog-earing a book or newspaper enough to see if it breaks off. Double folding is used to illustrate that paper lacks permanence, unlike digital media and microfilm. Baker maintains in his book that the view of paper's impermanence is a gross misconception propagated by such organizations as the National Endowment for the Humanities and the Library of Congress.

Double Fold presents this drama on a larger scale. It's not only about the bad decisions being made about book preservation, but it also brings to light the evils of bureaucracy and the ability of government autocrats to dupe some professional book people. *Double Fold* is no less creative or passionate than Baker's other works, and he is not above some borderline character assassination. Understandably, the professional library community was outraged. Ironically, they were more upset by Baker's challenge to the current preservation practices than by the subject matter of his other works, which include the phone-sex-laden *Vox* (1992), *The Fermata* (1994), whose narrator has the ability to stop time and have his naughty way with unsuspecting bosses, and *Checkpoint* (2004), where two men discuss assassinating President George W. Bush.

As one who went to graduate school in Information Sciences (which is the old Library Sciences, but we're taught not to use the antiquated L word), I spent quite a bit of time with library types, and a few of them can be rigid. However, librarians do get picked on. In modern times, librarian stereotyping originated with Frank Capra's *It's a Wonderful Life*, when Clarence the Angel shows George Bailey (Jimmy Stewart) what life in Bedford Falls would have been like if George hadn't survived a boyhood plunge into an icy pond. In the most ghastly scene of all, Bailey's wife, Mary (Donna Reed), is sentenced to a lonely existence at the circulation desk of the Pottersville Community Library.

No wonder librarians can become testy. Trained in the specifics of information organization and retrieval, they now spend a significant part of their workdays fixing paper jams and keeping teenage boys from surfing for pornography. Even a promotional campaign on Mattel's Barbie.com website, which asked Barbie fans to choose architect, librarian, or policewoman for the aging supermodel's next career change (she's had more career changes than I), failed to catapult the profession of book stewardship into a more favorable light. Print, television, and movie images continue to promote the stereo-

Bookselling Crime

Not only are booksellers a grumpy lot, but they have their share of evildoers as well. In 2004, a Nashville bookstore was the subject of a lengthy investigative article involving stolen books. A city-wide rash of bookstore thefts prompted a local newspaper to expose one bookstore's malfeasance. In the report, former employees and other book-store owners alleged that one store was purchasing books that had been stolen from other bookstores. Medical, nursing, and law books and boxed-set editions of *The Chronicles of Narnia* were appearing on shelves of the offending bookstore, some still in their shrink wrap. The article described in detail how these book deals "went down," including one transaction in a Blockbuster Video parking lot (further aggravating the crime in my opinion) between the owner and the grubby book thieves who were described as if they were miscreants from a Dickens novel. Apparently, it is not uncommon for books to go missing from libraries and end up in used book-stores. But one used bookstore ripping off another has taken the pre-owned book industry to further depths of depravity—if for no other reason than the false advertising of selling some new books as used.

type of book people as bespectacled, bunned, and in the words of one of my favorite information science professors, "always staring at their shoes." Not even an action figure of Seattle librarian and writer Nancy

Pearl, author of *Book Lust: Recommended Reading for Every Mood, Moment, and Reason* (2003), has been able to break the media's stranglehold on this stereotype. Maybe if Barbie and Ms. Pearl could wear the same clothes . . .

In another irony, a defense of the slightly antisocial nature of book people comes indirectly from Nicholson Baker himself, who includes a scene in *The Fermata* where the main character, Arno Stine, talks about using his special powers to keep people from wasting his time. "I question the right of anyone to waste our time," says Stine, who references the prolific sixteenth-century Italian mathematician Girolamo Cardano. "The wasting of time is an abomination." Maybe book people would rather be reading a good book, and everything else is, well, simply a waste of time. You have to admit, they should know what's worth reading.

This idea puts a whole new spin on the belief that book people are not outgoing and warm. I wouldn't go so far as to say that book people are rugged individualists who should be admired for their social honesty, and I think book people should have their license to read revoked if they are shepherding a substandard place like that bookstore in Allegan. Nevertheless, it does put a little more responsibility on us as book shoppers to raise the level of literary discourse. If you are at a complete loss as to what to say the next time you are being ignored at a bookstore, try interrupting the reader who is supposed to be working and asking what he or she thinks of that

smartass in *The Book Shopper* who says book people aren't friendly. It might not work, but just getting a book person to lift his or her nose out of the
pages and smile knowingly would be a major literary
achievement.

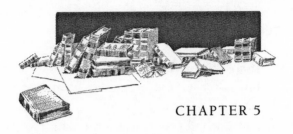

CHAPTER 5

Amazon Uncovered

To some, it must seem like heresy to mention Amazon.com when talking about book shopping. Should Amazon even be considered a bookstore, since it also sells appliances, garden accessories, and furniture? Well, who is to say what a bookstore should do just to stay alive. In *Cosmic Profit: How to Make Money Without Doing Time* (1979), Ray Mungo talks about the high expectations he had for the bookstore he opened in Seattle in 1973—"no Hallmark cards, junk fiction, stationery supplies, novelties, posters, bumper stickers"—and how he soon succumbed to market pressures just to keep afloat.* (Remember, Amazon opened its doors as the Earth's Biggest Bookstore in 1995.) Despite its wide range of non-book merchandise, Amazon is still our national, albeit virtual, bookstore, and it serves as an example of what I like and dislike about big-time book selling. I view being a book shopper on Amazon as just another of modern life's vicarious experiences, much

---

* For more about Ray Mungo, see Chapter 8, "Growing Old with the New Journalists."

like being a typical sports fan. As a Chicago Cubs fan, for example, I follow the sport, checking the results of the Cubs' efforts online, catching games on cable television, buying a team T-shirt. But rarely do I join other Cub masochists as a spectator at the friendly confines of Wrigley Field. Book shopping on Amazon is similar, although it takes you a step further. Most of us have surfed its website, bought something, and maybe even commented on a book in a review, without ever meeting another reader or the editors who monitor the website. So, despite there being no friendly confines to visit, Amazon is a nationally shared book shopping experience. To discuss book shopping without bringing up Amazon is like talking baseball without mentioning steroids.

For the conscientious book shopper, the relationship with Amazon is a complicated one. Initially, there is the guilt that supporting such a retail juggernaut is doing independent bookstores or independent used bookstores great harm. But after burying that guilt deep inside (where it belongs with other guilt), I can rationalize that I just want the book (whether it be used or new) without making the trek to a bookshop. Ordering online is the path of least resistance.*

---

* Just to clarify: Amazon has two avenues of shopping. Its regular website has brand new books with some decent discounts. It also has links where you can order used or remaindered books from a network of online used bookstores at drastically reduced prices (but you pay several dollars for shipping and wait for the book to arrive via USPS Media Mail).

Once this initial obstacle is overcome, there are other aspects to consider. When I buy a book sight unseen, much of my satisfaction depends on the degree of familiarity I have with the book. If it is a book I have already read and am just buying for a friend, there's not much uncertainty, but if it's a purchase based on a review (a dangerous endeavor) or a recommendation by a colleague (equally reckless), then the chances of buyer's remorse are greater. Buying unfamiliar books online is a kind of gamble, albeit only a small one. At least books are relatively inexpensive impulse items, and they don't take up a lot of room—unlike power boats or home exercise equipment.

The problem with buying used books online, however, isn't that the books arrive with torn pages or smeared in yellow highlighter. Amazon's used booksellers (who often have brick-and-mortar stores as well) are usually good about describing the condition of their books. What makes the online experience so unfulfilling is the lack of opportunity for perusal, the decreased chances of a serendipitous encounter, and the good feeling that comes with delayed gratification.

For those of us who want to do a lot of perusing in a short time, the physical space of a bookstore works to our advantage. I can scan a bookshelf chock full of books in a minute or two, which I can't do on the Internet no matter how speedy my connection. If I see a book that interests me, I can pull the book from the shelf and give the table of contents, the index (if nonfiction), and several paragraphs the quick once over, taking special note of the author's style, which is a major selling point for me. (Admittedly, I can easily get sucked in by flair or clarity.) This cannot be done for most books in Amazon's catalog. Sure, a few of the more recent titles offer a look at the table of contents or a chapter or two (the publishers pay for these, right?), but most of Amazon's older offerings do not include previews.

I often discover a new book while browsing a store's shelves. One time when I was at a used bookstore picking up a copy of Barbara Kingsolver's *Poisonwood Bible* (1998) for my niece, I stumbled across a mint-condition, first-edition hardback copy of Maxine Hong Kingston's *The Fifth Book of Peace* (2003) for twenty dollars. That's more than I usually pay for a used book, but I rationalized the expense in several ways. I had other Kingston books in hardback, and *The Fifth Book of Peace* would be a fine addition to my collection.* Moreover, that particular bookstore was one of my favorites and I wanted to support them whenever I could.

Physically, the Kingston book was impressive. There was not a mark on it except the price lightly inscribed in pencil. It had a clear protective cover over the dust jacket. The paper was crisp and hadn't yellowed. There was no danger of pages coming

* For more about Maxine Hong Kinston, see Chapter 7, "Prerequisites: What Every Good Used Bookstore Should Have."

loose, since the binding was sewn and not glued. None of the Amazon used-book descriptions provide this kind of detail. Had I not visited the store, I would never have stumbled upon this Kingston gem. This kind of fortuitous discovery is not uncommon. Besides finding first-rate copies of books by authors I already like, I also find new books that somehow inexplicably resonate—and these experiences are available to me only in the physical space of a store.

Then there is the pleasure of delayed gratification. There are some books that I choose to wait for at a reduced price rather than buy online or at a major book retailer as soon as they are published. This was the case with Richard Ford's most recent offering, *The Lay of the Land* (2006), his sequel to *Independence Day* (1995).* I knew that as soon as the book went into paperback, hardcovers would be available at reduced prices. Imagine my extra tweak of joy at paying only half price at a local independent bookstore. I waited, and my faith that I would find a bargain did not go unrewarded. Such is the additional buzz that comes with playing the market.

Besides the watered-down purchasing experience, another downside to Amazon's service is the implicit perception that all the information on the site is accurate. In general, I do find the information there useful, and hardly a week goes by when I'm

* For more about Richard Ford, see Chapter 9, "Big Social Book Shopping Novels."

not accessing its site, trying to pull up the name of a forgotten author or the title of a book. (No wonder reference librarians have become the loneliest people in town.) Nevertheless, I treat the product information about the book, the reviews, and the recommendations with skepticism. It's not that I think Amazon is being deceptive or incompetent, but rather I think we as book shopping consumers sometimes forget that our National Bookstore has one prime directive—to sell books.

It is quite easy to misinterpret Amazon's shopping catalog as a library catalog. For example, to check the original publishing date of Maxine Hong Kingston's *China Men* requires scrolling through Amazon's offerings of ten different publications of the book. The dates listed in these books are the release dates of later *China Men* editions rather than the original publication date. If you're not careful, you may think that *China Men* was published in 1989 instead of its original publication year of 1980. While consumer ignorance is not Amazon's fault, their website does tend to support an often false impression of the scope of the company's expertise.

Another of Amazon's annoying aspects is the way it acts like your book shopper buddy. Whenever you buy anything online, you leave yourself open to being bombarded by ads for a host of similar products, and Amazon has been doing this for a long time. After you buy a book, expect to receive computer-generated notices to buy more of the same type of book. Once, I bought a golf book for my brother, and for awhile every time a new golf book came out, Amazon pitched it to me, even though I've abstained from all books about the sport ever since I was forced to read and review the abominable *Legend of Bagger Vance* (1995). Although Amazon offers a link where I can tell them that I bought the book as a gift instead of for myself, I choose to remain silent. If I supply this information, Amazon will shove what they perceive to be more enticing titles at me while updating my purchasing preferences. (The corporate world may already have a jaded view of my consumer profile, since I'm always filling out my product warranty cards as if I were a physician making fifteen thousand dollars a year whose hobbies are cooking and taxidermy.)

Amazon's marketing methods are not nearly as disturbing to me as a trickier and more misleading aspect of Amazon, namely, the book reviews. My initial complaint is that most of Amazon's book reviewers get paid absolutely nothing for their time, thought, and effort, which is the same pay scale offered by many newspapers.* But in the case of Amazon, you rarely even receive the book *gratis*; you've already purchased and supposedly read the book. And forget about any authorship rights for the re-

---

* See the arguments presented for paying reviewers in Chapter 3, "A Reviewer's Lament."

viewer. The statement about the rights to any work you submit doesn't sound promising for anyone but Amazon:

> If you do post content or submit material, and unless we indicate otherwise, you grant Amazon a nonexclusive, royalty-free, perpetual, irrevocable, and fully sublicensable right to use, reproduce, modify, adapt, publish, translate, create derivative works from, distribute, and display such content throughout the world in any media.

Although reviewers may retain rights to their own words, Amazon has paid nothing for the "community of customers to help sell more of its books."* Also, if you wrote a clever, pithy review that contained a newly minted book lovers' phrase along the lines of "Too Many Books and Not Enough Time" or "I'd Rather Be Reading Bukowski," then Amazon could mass-market it on a T-shirt and not pay you anything. Or let's say that, because of your reviews, you became a kind of an Amazonian celebrity, a virtual Brian Lamb, so to speak. Amazon has every right to repurpose your reviews into a book of its own, again paying you nothing. I have no verifiable knowledge that this has been done, or that Amazon would think of such things, but the point I'm making here is once you've sent your review to Amazon, it may still be yours, but it's theirs, too.

---

* *NPR Morning Edition* (February 11, 2008), "Bookseller Amazon Building on Review Function."

These downsides have not impeded me from being among the thousands of Amazon reviewers who submit their thoughts about certain books. After all, I do meet *all* the requirements to be a reviewer, which are, in the words of Amazon: "Customers! Anyone who has purchased items from Amazon and is in good standing in the Amazon community can create reviews." In other words, I have joined the throng of scholars, coffee baristas, parking lot attendants, personal friends or lifelong enemies of the author, and submitted my views about a book to Amazon. It doesn't matter whether I read a book a year or a book a day, as long as I am "in good standing in the Amazon community."

I do have my standards, however, and I will only consider doing a review if I can be the inaugural reviewer, as I was for Leonard Michaels's *The Men's Club* (1981)* and Kim Trevathan's *Paddling the Tennessee River: A Voyage on Easy Water* (2001). (See the Bookmark "Damn Yankee Reviewers" at the end of this chapter.) At least being the first reviewer gives a voice to previously silent books, while giving oneself a tiny bit of cachet (fame at last!), as opposed to being the 3,000th reviewer (I'm not exaggerating) for *Harry Potter and the Deathly Hallows* (2007). Actually, I'm a little confused why someone would

---

* As I recall, one reason I wrote the review was that Amazon used to offer a fifty-dollar gift certificate for the "Review of the Day," a practice they have since abandoned.

like to be the 3,000th person to review a Harry Potter book. What possible nuance could this reviewer add to what has been written hundreds of times? I am also perplexed by those dedicated reviewers who have commented on thousands of books and movies. Admittedly, there is the lure of "contributing something to the world of books and words" (explained earlier in Chapter 3, "A Reviewer's Lament"), so how can I criticize them too harshly? I understand that this need to contribute is part of our longing for a sense of community, but the Amazon community is impoverished and may even prevent people from seeking out other, more nourishing communities.

For me—and this may be a generational thing—community is when I go to a bagel shop and the owner knows what I want, or I'm at the local mechanic and he knows the history of my car without looking at a printout. There are not many non-denominational places left that can give us this sense of belonging. Fortunately, used and independent bookstores are often those kinds of places, where if you frequent them enough, the owners do eventually recognize you. They may not know your name, but they know your dust jacket (face). Even then, it may take a few visits before I'll start to chit-chat about books, because as you know, the proprietors and employees at these places are usually introverted.

My complaint about Amazon is that it deals in illusions: the aforementioned illusion of community and the illusion that, by participating, the customer is contributing to the culture. Amazon is hardly alone in doing this. Newspapers with blogs (replacing the more traditional letter to the editor), websites for television programs, and sports radio talk show hosts who read email on the air all operate under the same guise. Participation seems democratic, of course, but this is assuming these efforts have any impact. David Granger, editor-in-chief of *Esquire*, made a bold, Emperor-Has-No-Clothes kind of statement in his April 2007 editor's column when he wrote, "The new opiate of the masses is the illusion of participation in the culture." As I understand Granger's comments, he is admitting how the larger publishing and entertainment companies view participatory content. To the publisher, free content from blogs, email messages, and postings are an opportunity for the placing of banner and popup ads rather than a center for meaningful dialogue.

With all this in mind, it's ironic that Amazon's behemoth nature does both the greatest service and disservice to the reading community. On the one hand, hard-to-locate books can now be found and purchased with ease. These books remain in circulation instead of being discarded. That is a good thing. On the other hand, Amazon promotes the illusion of community and participation in the culture in order to entice you to spend more time in its online catalog. So before spending *all* your time and money at Amazon, you may want to rethink your actions. Ask yourself, what am I searching for today? Do I want a

Damn Yankee Reviewers

In my discussion of Amazon, I suggest that posted reviews could be part of a buddy system of writers doing favorable reviews of their friends' books. I know firsthand of one such conspiracy—my review of Kim Trevathan's *Paddling the Tennessee River*. Kim currently teaches at Maryville College in Maryville, Tennessee. In our previous lives we worked together during the halcyon days of the dot.com era. I wanted to honor our friendship by reading his book and at least writing something for Amazon. (Kim had nothing to do with this.) I decided before reading the opening paragraph that I would give the book the same treatment as I would any other. The sole exception would be that if I *didn't like it*, I wouldn't write anything. This wasn't an issue, since the book was fine, but I'm going to send you to Amazon to read the review rather than repeat it here.

Reviewing Kim's second book, *Coldhearted River: A Canoe Odyssey Down the Cumberland* (2006), about navigating the Cumberland River, was more problematic. In this book, I make a cameo appearance as part of the team that dropped Kim and a photographer off at the river's source in destitute and violent Harlan County, Kentucky. I come off as a smart-mouthed Yankee who incessantly cracks *Deliverance* jokes and adds to Kim's nervousness about the trip. (Southerners like Kim think of Yanks as anyone born north of the Ohio River.) For the record, since I make an appearance in his book, I held off writing a review. Call it professional ethics, garden-variety laziness, or what it really was—

bruised feelings stemming from a proud Midwesterner's oversensitivity to being labeled a Yankee.

convenient way to buy a book, or do I need to connect to another book person? If it's the latter, you
might have a better book shopping experience if you
pull yourself away from the keyboard and head out
to your neighborhood bookstore.

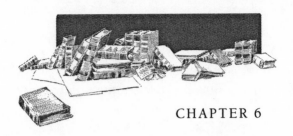

CHAPTER 6

Master Control: The Influences of a Book Shopper Friend

I'M NOT THE PRIMAL book shopper, nor am I the ultimate book shopper. Those distinctions belong to my longtime friend Dave, who taught me that haunting used bookstores not only allows me to pay less (heightening my reading pleasure), but it also offers a second chance, namely, the opportunity to discover that many books deserve another look. Book shoppers like books that feature eclectic writing styles, or capture a specific time or place or emotion (a unique vision, as Eudora Welty puts it), or have a driving plot that is neither predictable nor hackneyed. For over twenty-five years, Dave has showered me with examples of such books. I've sent a trickle of recommendations back his way, but compared to Dave, I am still a neophyte book shopper.

We met at a National Public Radio affiliate station in east central Illinois in 1979, when I was hired as the night board operator. Dave, a student at the University of Illinois at the time, got stuck with the job of training me. Depending on the production schedule, we'd work together, monitoring pre-recorded broadcasts of both the AM and FM affiliates from a soundproof room known as Master Control. As operators, our shifts could be maddeningly busy as we ran news feeds, taped music for rebroadcast, and helped announcers with their production. At other times we could be working by ourselves playing endless symphonies and chamber pieces. Borrowing the marketing blurb from the blockbuster movie at the time, *Alien*, Master Control was the place where "no one can hear you scream."

Dave trained me on the intricacies of Ampex reel-to-reel tape decks, turntables, and the correct positioning of microphones. Our station manager was extremely picky about who was allowed on the air, and Dave and I lacked the deep, sophisticated voices needed to be NPR announcers. We weren't allowed on-air except in an emergency—when a tornado or flood or clouds of corn-eating grasshoppers descended upon our listeners. One benefit of the job was that there was ample time for conversation. Dave and I developed a kind of oral tradition, which included talking about books.

With a personal style that was encyclopedic, instructive, and tinged with humor, Dave introduced me to many writers. He could recite Henry Miller's *Tropic of Capricorn* (1939) like it was a nursery rhyme, with such favorite lines as "We were a merry crew, united in our desire to f—k the company at all costs," and "It was a slaughterhouse, so help me God . . . a waste of men, material and effort." Both passages are references to Miller's experiences with the Cosmodemonic Telegraph Company of North America (Western Union in the 1920s), and the passages would later be signature quotes for my own thoughts about the world of work. Miller's description of the corporate churn policies of hiring and firing low-paid employees all in the name of profits reminds us how little has changed over the last eighty years.

Dave located a hardback copy of *Tropic of Capricorn* for me at the campus YMCA used bookstore for $2.50, and I still have it. Later he gave me a cheap copy of Miller's biography, *Always Merry and Bright* (1978) by Jay Martin. I understand why people think Miller was a filthy-mouthed misogynist (his liberal use of the c-word), but if you look closer at his life and his art you realize that his "vulgarity" was just part of his literary persona.* Both *Tropics* (*Tropic of Cancer* was published in 1934) are unparalleled in their manic energy and robustness. They are books for restless youth, but I'm always hesitant to recommend them to young adults (especially my daughters) because of the threat of sending them down

---

* In *Critical Essays on Henry Miller* (1992), Ronald Gottesman collected articles and letters about the legacy of Miller. Erica Jong of *Fear of Flying* (1973) fame wrote an entire book about Miller entitled *The Devil at Large: Erica Jong on Henry Miller* (1993). The Jong book is easier to find than the Gottesman. My stained copy of the Gottesman book came from my daughter, who rescued it from a pile of discarded books on a Cambridge, Massachusetts, curb.

the path of promiscuity, irresponsibility, and rampant bohemianism. Reading Miller was something I did when I was young and just out of college. It was what I did instead of traveling abroad.

Dave also pointed me to Louis-Ferdinand Céline's books of the 1930s, *Journey to the End of the Night* (1932) and the book with the all-time best title (if you enjoy despair), *Death on the Installment Plan* (1936). *Journey* is a semi-autobiographical account of a man's nightmarish travels in West Africa, New York, and Detroit. *Death* is an account of the childhood of the same narrator in the slums of Paris. Both were written in an elliptical style of outrage with graphic descriptions of the narrator's most unsavory thoughts. Later Dave gave me one of the grittiest books of all time, Hubert Selby Jr.'s *Last Exit to Brooklyn* (1964). *Exit* is a collection of character-based stories set in the seamier side of post–World War II New York City. One unforgettable story recounts the rise and fall of the promiscuous teenager Tralala, who is eventually gang-raped and murdered. Another tells the sorry tale of an unemployed father living in the projects, who drinks and leaves his infant kids in their own filth behind baby crib bars while his wife is at work. Dave summed up thoughts about Selby in his own review inscribed on the inside cover: "It ain't pretty, but it is one hell of a book."

Despite our surface allegiances to these authors writing on the raw edges of life, we were mild-mannered fellows whose only anarchist fantasies centered on taking the station hostage and broadcasting the Rutles (Eric Idle's Python-like spoof of the Beatles) or our own lame satire called "Air Piracy" ("From the files of the FCCC, the Federal Communications Crime Commission . . ."). Curiously, our satire proved ineffectual, soliciting not a single comment from the management or the listening audience. Little did we know then that throughout the years we would remain as we were at the station— good citizen anarchists.

Dave eventually moved to Seattle, where he worked as a technical writer and married the poet-writer Laurie Blauner. Her book *Somebody* (2003) is autobiographical fiction about her relationship with her mother, whom Dave refers to as the oldest living party girl, and with Dave. Laurie has a poet's command of the language, and she captures Dave's looks and personality perfectly in just a few words. Of course, she mentions the books in his study: "Books are everywhere. In high piles, stacked buildings about to topple over."

I've made it to Seattle a couple of times to visit them. Seattle is a great book town. Not only does it have the monstrous, new glass-and-steel Seattle Public Library (whose poor acoustics, as Dave says, "make the place feel and sound like an airport terminal"), but there are many enticing used bookstores throughout the city. Dave and Laurie have hauled me around in their 1996 Crown Victoria, covering bookstores from the Elliott Bay Book Company in the old red-light district to the University of Washington, where there are several top used bookstores within walking distance of the campus. At one establishment, Dave had a thousand dollars worth of bookstore credit, and he turned me loose on the place, carte blanche. Despite his generosity, I blew my trip budget badly and ended up with so many books that Dave (who has a love of gadgetry that includes a used box-making machine) was kind enough to package and ship them home to me.

Laurie has a quiet, easygoing demeanor, which belies her intensity as a writer, and she is no slouch herself in her knowledge of books. While shopping, she introduced me to a book of twelve short stories by Amy Bloom called *Come to Me* (1993).* Even though Bloom was up for the National Book Award, I had never heard of her. Bloom is a psychotherapist, and she maintains that her stories are not about her patients, but the influence is there and underlies her descriptions of her characters and their behaviors. My favorite in the collection is "Psychoanalysis Changed My Life," a wistful story about a divorced, middle-aged patient who finds new romance with the help of her dying therapist.

Laurie also put me on to Michael Chabon's *The Amazing Adventures of Kavalier & Clay* (2000), and I will always appreciate that. It's the story of two cartoonist cousins drawing and grinding their way to the top of the publishing world in a romanticized pre–World War II New York City. It reads fast,

---

* Bloom has since written the bestselling novel *Away* (2007). I set it aside after fifty pages.

with every chapter moving like a comic book serial. Each day or chapter, you get a little cliffhanger of an adventure, and it's easy to get into Chabon's rhythm. His detail about the comic book industry during those times is equally impressive.

During one Seattle visit, Dave gave me his personal tour of The Vintage Telephone Equipment Museum (now The Museum of Communications), where he volunteers with several retired phone company employees to preserve every conceivable aspect of the phone company culture. The museum collection includes phones, a British phone booth, switchboards, walls of routing systems (which the volunteers have maintained in working order), telephone poles with crossarms festooned with wires and insulators, and teletype machines like the ones we used to work with at the radio station back in Illinois. Completing the experience, the museum was populated with incorrigible phone company retirees not unlike Henry Miller's Cosmodemonic sidekicks Hymie and O'Rourke ("a prince of man") from *Tropic of Capricorn*.

We also visited Dave's current passion, a voice-recording studio he built himself called Full-Track Productions, where "recordings are made with plain and simple old-fashioned monaural goodness." Dave took the lucrative downsizing buyouts he received from his employers at Microsoft and Hewlett-Packard and wisely invested them in the studio, which can make top-quality voice recordings and output to analog open-reel tape or digital compact disc. Inside the recording booth we listened to a copy of "Air

The Philip Roth Book Shopper

Dave was always a big Philip Roth fan, and considering Roth's output, he is the best qualified to write The Philip Roth Book Shopper. If he did, he could include his anecdote about attending a Roth reading in Seattle in 1993:

"I wanted to tell you that I had the privilege of hearing Philip Roth speak a few months ago. There's a literary lecture series that typically brings eight to ten big names to town each year; in previous years, I've heard Andrei Codrescu (a great storyteller and quite a character) and Robert Bly (not all that impressive; the consummate bullshit artist in my humble opinion).

"Roth read selections from *Patrimony* [1991] and entertained written questions from the audience—which was enormous, by the way. Nearly every seat in the house was filled (this was a large church in downtown Seattle). I'd say there were at least 1,500 or 2,000 people. I was somewhat surprised; I wasn't sure he had such a following out here on the West Coast, though it did look like an older crowd.

"As much as I hate to chase after autographs, I packed a small clothbound Modern Library edition of *Goodbye, Columbus and Five Short Stories* [1966] in my jacket pocket. Roth was pretty exhausted from either a grueling schedule or a long airplane ride (possibly both), and hence didn't read very long or answer too many questions, though he was very polite in answering even the most pedestrian ones. (They picked them out of a hat, more or less.)

"After the presentation, Roth stepped down to the front of the crowd and shook a few hands and signed a few (a very few) books. You had to be quick on this, and I didn't quite get down there in time. Just as his handlers were hustling him out the exit I called to him. 'Mr. Roth,' I said (the entourage quickly sized me up to see if I was a psychopathic obsessive fan or just a Seattle guy in a green Goretex raincoat), 'my father went to Weequahic High School.' At that, he smiled and asked what year and my father's name. It turns out (though I had known this) that my father is about five years older than Roth, though he said perhaps his older brother Sandy might remember my father since they were only a year apart. (My father graduated in 1945 and Sandy Roth graduated in 1946.) Weequahic High School and the Weequahic section of Newark figure prominently, as you may recall, in many of Roth's books.

"I asked if he might sign my book, and he said fine, though he had to make it quick, as he had to be moving on. (Boy, those handlers were really efficient.)"

Piracy" from our salad days. It was embarrassingly amateurish. Fortunately we were in a room where no one could hear us scream.

I cannot overstate the influence Dave has had on my development as a reader and a book shopper. Part of it has been his steady friendship and his subtle enthusiasm for books. From a distance, I see how words in all their guises have guided his life—words written and spoken by others, including the woman he married, as well as his own work as a technical writer. Essentially *The Book Shopper* attempts to do for you what Dave has done for me. Every chapter is a day trip to a different world—to a place where it's okay to be quirky and passionate about things and a half beat off the lockstep of contemporary culture. Dave is the original book shopper; this book is the second.

PART TWO

Acquisitions

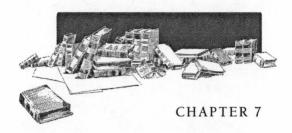

CHAPTER 7

Prerequisites: What Every Good Bookstore Should Have

IN ADDITION TO THE standard black-and-white kitty cat that rubs against your legs while you're browsing and the quiet, intensely intelligent, mousy girl in a worn sweater who works the register, there are certain ingredients that all respectable used bookstores should have.* Even more important than the deep, calming drone of some National Public Radio announcer over the bookstore speakers, there are certain books—and I'm not talking about the usual classics, but the books of several contemporary writers—that I expect all decent used bookstores to carry. Seeing these authors on the shelves immediately tells me what kind of establishment I am in and whether I'll be exiting shortly or taking off the rest of the afternoon to do some serious book shopping.

---

* The male version of the standard mousy girl is the rustic, handsome, but sullen guy. Both employees are in need of money.

These are the same set of books I associate with my first happy experiences of book shopping. I didn't pay more than a couple of dollars for any of them, and I thought each was of extraordinary value. They are books by the authors who started me on this whole obsession, and whether they are universally accepted in the canons of contemporary literature I leave for someone else to determine. Over the years, reading and rereading parts of them has continued to entertain and sustain me.

Everybody likes a list, even if only to see if they agree with it. The only order to the one that follows is alphabetical, and it is important to note that even though I admire each of these authors, I recognize that writers have uneven careers. This was pointed out by Larry McMurtry in his 1999 book of essays, *Walter Benjamin at the Dairy Queen: Reflections at Sixty and Beyond*. McMurtry noted that inconsistency is a characteristic of most writers, including himself.

Pat Barker: Therapy

Regeneration (1991) is the first book of Pat Barker's World War I trilogy, which also includes *The Eye in the Door* (1993) and *The Ghost Road* (1995). Rather than focus primarily on battlefield events, Barker views the war from behind the lines—at Craiglockhart War Hospital in Scotland. At Craiglockhart, the brilliant psychiatrist Dr. William Rivers treats a host of patients with "tics and twitches," including Siegfried Sassoon, the noted poet and war hero who publicly refused to stay at the front. Faced with disgracing a popular hero, the British war machine transfers Sassoon to Rivers's care, where the doctor must determine whether the war is insane or Sassoon is insane for saying it is.

Another major character-patient is Billy Prior, a smart, tough, working-class lad who not only has suffered on the battlefield (a comrade's eyeball ended up in his hand), but who is also victimized by British class distinctions and prejudices. Prior becomes a more important character in *The Eye in the Door* and *The Ghost Road*.

Regeneration was a breakthrough book for me—I had been unable to read anything of any length in the months following my trench warfare-like separation and divorce from my wife. I was still in therapy, working on deep-seated personal conflicts that I wasn't really aware of until I had one of those sobbing sessions where I discovered the truth about my situation. As I slowly recovered, my mind would drift easily and printed words were just black shapes on white paper. I had never before experienced such an inability to read. Several well-intentioned friends recommended fluffy escapist material, but eventually I saw on my shelf a book with a promising title, *Regeneration*—the need to "create a new, especially an improved state."

In the novel, which is based on actual people and events, the compassionate but dutiful Rivers sees patient-soldiers who have survived physically but have been mentally destroyed by their experiences in the war. Instead of presenting battlefield panoramas, Barker chooses brief scenes of unimaginable psychological horror—the kind that eventually triggers a soldier's breakdown—to capture the magnitude of the slaughter. Rivers explains these triggering moments as being not single, isolated events, but the accumulated weight of a series of stresses. He says to one of his patients, "You're thinking of breakdown as a reaction to a single traumatic event, but it's not like that. It's more a matter of . . . *erosion*. Weeks and months of stress in a situation where you can't get away from it."

Admittedly, divorce is *not* like being in the trenches (I say that now), but I found many of the metaphors in the book relevant to my life at the time. Basically, Barker understands the nature of pain. In one scene, she describes Rivers's prewar work with another doctor, Henry Head, who is experimenting with nerve regeneration. Rivers observes that the nerves Head is trying to re-grow are extremely sensitive. The slightest stimulus causes unbearable pain to the patient. That observation spans our mental as well as our physical states. The parts of our psyche we are trying to re-grow in psychotherapy are extremely vulnerable to any stimulus. I imagine this is a dilemma for mental health practitioners. They know the places they must go are by far the most painful to their patients, but they also know that without going there, patients have no hope of healing.

Barker followed *Regeneration* with *The Eye in the Door* and *The Ghost Road*. The former includes several characters from *Regeneration*, but the emphasis shifts from the treating of patients at Craiglockhart to the insanity on the home front. Billy Prior has been reassigned to the Ministry of Munitions and ordered to infiltrate and investigate citizens who are opposed to the war. One of the female conspirators, unjustly accused of plotting to assassinate Prime Minister David Lloyd George, is a woman from Prior's old neighborhood who helped raise him for a year when his own mother was ill with tuberculosis. The war is already in its third bloody year, and it isn't going well. But rather than blame the reckless military commanders, the government focuses on anyone remotely dissident—particularly pacifists (known as "conchies") and homosexuals. Prior must sort out truth from paranoia, a task made tougher by his conflicting allegiances and brief recurring bouts of amnesia.

In the aftermath of the September 11th terrorist attacks, *The Eye in the Door* has become even more relevant. We in America have seen the lengths to which a government will go to control dissidents in the guise of combating terrorism. One may believe Great Britain is a reasonably civilized Western country (we've learned that from *Masterpiece Theatre*, haven't we?), but Barker shows how those opposed to the war were often beaten and imprisoned. In one case, a pacifist was placed naked in a cold cell (sounds like Abu Ghraib) with only a military uniform offered for clothing. Of course, we Americans also think of our country as morally advanced, but the Patriot Act, the disgrace at Abu Ghraib, the treatment of POWs at Guantanamo, and the rantings against the "sexual orientation" of SpongeBob SquarePants have many of us thinking otherwise.

In *The Ghost Road*, Barker shifts the narrative between Rivers's work at Craiglockhart and Prior's return to the front in time for the full-scale Allied offensive in the fall of 1918. A final battle scene captures the futile bravery of life at the front, but Barker keeps the writing tight and meaningful—perhaps in homage to the poets Sassoon and Wilfred Owen, who were patients at Craiglockhart; Owen was in the same unit as Prior.

While I still appreciate *Regeneration* as the breakthrough book that ended my I-don't-feel-like-reading funk, I am even more impressed the more I look at these three books together. Although critics are aware of Barker, many readers know little about her, and I recommend her work as frequently as that of any author. The books work on so many levels—as fiction, as social history, and perhaps most important for me, as reminders of the value of therapy. Victory over suffering is not always possible, but even if we only achieve armistice, we can at least step back and begin to see the complex nature of our own psyches and then begin to regenerate.*

---

* The film *Behind the Lines* is based on Barker's trilogy. It stars Jonathan Pryce (*Brazil, Pirates of the Caribbean*) as Rivers. It's a solid movie, faithful in tone and spirit, but like most cinematic adaptations, incomplete.

Julian Barnes: Understanding Aging

Julian Barnes is the author of one of my all-time favorite cheapies, *Staring at the Sun* (1986). This book was critically acclaimed (I still have a yellowed copy of Carlos Fuentes's review in the *New York Times*), and the paperback edition was available for years by the truckload at low, low prices. Set in modern Britain, *Staring at the Sun* tells the story of an ordinary woman, Jean, who seeks the world's truths. From her childhood in the 1920s, she experiences small miracles in her travels and in her daily routine. In her advancing age, Jean muses about whether her life has been good, bad, or wasted. She debunks a male gerontologist who tries to demonstrate to people what it's like to be old by stuffing cotton wool in their ears, putting pebbles in their shoes, and smearing Vaseline on their glasses. The trouble with this idea of "instant aging," as Jean points out, is that we age slowly. It's not an overnight phenomenon. Furthermore, we age in other people's eyes long before we admit to old age ourselves.

One of the reasons I like this book so much—and I don't often let on about this—is that in the early 1980s I returned to school briefly for a master's in gerontology. It was one of those sidetracks we sometimes take in our lives that don't pan out or lead to a specific job, but I always felt it was a beneficial part of my education. There may be an advantage in knowing what to expect before one ages or in understanding how other cultures view aging differently or in accepting that the insecurities of growing old are not unique to our generation. I won't know if I've aged well until I'm dead, so maybe Barnes's light-hearted course on the subject is a better use of one's time than seeking out an advanced degree.*

On the downside, I liked *Staring at the Sun* so much that I purchased bargain copies of Barnes's *Metroland* (1980) and *Flaubert's Parrot* (1984). I found the first a dull coming-of-age novel while the second only revealed the gaping holes in my knowledge of Gustave Flaubert. Again, consistency can be a problem with a novelist and, without wanting to sound immodest, a good reason to have *The Book Shopper* as a handy companion.

Nevertheless, there is another book by Barnes worth grabbing—though I rarely see it—*A History of the World in 10½ Chapters* (1989). In this collection of short stories, Barnes writes about such things as a termite's view of Noah's Ark, maritime mishaps, and my favorite, an account of what it's like to be in heaven. Every day is a perfect day in heaven, where every morning the servant brings you a perfect breakfast, including a sweet pink grapefruit, "not yellow, and each segment had already been carefully freed from its clinging membrane." Of course, there is the problem of celestial monotony (everything being so perfect) and the disappointment of finding out that everyone gets through the pearly

* Apparently Barnes is still grappling with mortality, as evidenced by his latest book, *Nothing to Be Frightened Of* (2008), a (nonfiction) meditation on death.

gates, even Hitler. Barnes's story is a perfect, logical scenario that replaces the dreams about heaven as a place where the streets are lined with gold and the days are filled with leisure. Having read it, you have to think about what happens after you get there. *A History of the World in 10½ Chapters* is also an example of one of my watchwords: If a collection's price is reduced enough, then it's worth buying for just one very good story.

T. Coraghessan Boyle: Hip and Hippies

I became acquainted with T. C. Boyle's writing when book shopper Dave sent me copies of some short stories with strange-sounding titles like "Bloodfall" and "A Women's Restaurant." The author's name was missing, but the stories, the first about a thunderstorm that rains blood and the second about a guy trying to sneak into a women's-only restaurant, stuck in my mind. This experience remained in mental mothballs for a couple of years until I began reading a funny, hip novel called *Budding Prospects: A Pastoral* (1984) about an inept marijuana grower's shelving "the whole hippie ethic—beads, beards, brotherhood, the community of man," for the pursuit of the real American dream, "money, Money, and nothing else." As I read this book, I recognized the thick, wacky descriptions decorated with strange words such as "algolagnic" as coming from the same author who wrote the stories Dave had sent me.

At last count, Boyle has written eleven novels and eight collections of short stories. Most of his novels, such as *A Friend of the Earth* (2000), *The Tortilla Curtain* (1995), and *Budding Prospects*, share the disturbing pattern of starting out gangbusters for 100 to 150 pages and then just petering out. A few, such as *East Is East* (1991), *The Road to Wellville* (1993), and *Riven Rock* (1998), limp along and never rise to any kind of apex in the first place. In many of his novels, such as the aforementioned *Friend* and *Budding Prospects*, along with one of his later efforts, *Drop City* (2003), Boyle is preoccupied with hippies or counterculture types who have gone astray. I would agree that there is nothing sadder than an old hippie, but it is hardly a topic that merits such a corpus of work. The major exception to all of Boyle's shortcomings as a novelist is *World's End* (1987), which is a great novel. (See the Bookmark "World's End.")

Part of Boyle's problem is his relentless desire for "hipness," which extends way beyond the author's goatee, eccentric dress, and University of Southern California professorship. His kind of writing is sometimes referred to as "wickedly funny," which is just another term for cynical. Although one never has enough colorful phases to spew out to describe a hangover ("as if his head were a radio caught between stations" or "his head had collapsed like a rotten jack-o-lantern"), Boyle's pyrotechnics have a tendency to burn out over the course of a novel.

Boyle's burnout style is less of a problem in his short stories. It's easier to dazzle for 15 pages than for 350. Some of Boyle's stories are dark, comic spins on society's latest preoccupations, such as "Hard Sell," an outdated but memorable piece about a public relations whiz who's been asked to soften the image of the Ayatollah Khomeini. "Hard Sell," "Bloodfall," and "A Women's Restaurant" are collected in *T. C. Boyle Stories*, along with several of my Boyle favorites:

- "Descent of Man," the story of the boyfriend of a primate researcher named Jane who discovers that she is leaving him to run away with one of her apes.
- The TV-script like "Heart of a Champion," about the day Lassie decides to abandon little "corn-silked hair, corn-fed faced" Timmy in favor of a scrawny, wild-eyed, but free-spirited coyote.
- "If the River Was Whiskey," a no-nonsense piece about the breakup of a family because of alcoholism. Boyle is especially graphic about alcoholics—their sallow skin and puffy eyes, and their lies. (Walter Van Brunt's father in *World's End* and Eddie Kane in *Riven Rock* come to mind also.)
- "Filthy with Things" skewers people who become obsessed with having things, owning things, and acquiring more things.

Boyle is a quintessential book shopper's writer. He's published a large body of work of varying price and quality, and his later works are more readily available at reduced prices because his reputation exceeds his sales.

World's End

Part of what makes a book great is the receptive nature of the reader at the time the book is encountered. Certainly this was my situation with T. C. Boyle's *World's End*, the sad saga of the cursed Van Brunt family, who along with their blood-related Native American kin were betrayed and kicked around throughout their family history at the hands of the Dutch, or more precisely, the Dutch who immigrated to America.

I found this book at a mall discount table while I was living in Holland, Michigan, near the breezy eastern shores of Lake Michigan. This is a city known for its gorgeous Tulip Time festival, scenic downtown, a strange ritual known as wooden shoe dancing, and some of the most passive-aggressive people you never want to meet. I lived there for three years in the early 1990s, adapting to its falsely congenial life, but ever mindful that if you were not a scion of Dutch ancestry you were a second-class citizen. The popular local bumper sticker, which read, IF YOU'RE NOT DUTCH, YOU'RE NOT MUCH, was not a joke; it was the community motto. This judgmental group, no matter how devoutly religious its members, had an institutional contempt for all non-Dutch people, except when it came to taking their money. Basically I learned to survive by socializing with non-Dutch residents or the occasionally refreshing anti-Dutch Dutch citizen. *World's End*'s story of subterfuge helped confirm for me the prejudices I was up against.

Of course the strength of *World's End* is more than its Dutch-bashing. It's a tale of how the pow-

erful perpetuate their control over the less fortunate in society. It's also a lesson on the influence of
history, especially family history. We are all more
or less "haunted, however haphazardly, by ghosts
of the past," writes Boyle. The book's main character, Walter Van Brunt, is affected not only by the
power structure of the community fathers but also
by the sins and character flaws of his own father.

Toward the end of the book, Walter's father
explains the family's sick history: "It's in the blood,
Walter, it's in the bones." Words that contain
truth—but how much truth is a question that can
be answered only by great fiction.

Bruce Duffy: Philosophy Made Easier

Bruce Duffy's novel *The World As I Found It* (1987) is
a fictional account of the life of philosopher Ludwig
Wittgenstein and his professional relationships with
his Cambridge colleagues Bertrand Russell and G. E.
Moore. Duffy explains in the book's preface that his
account is fundamentally accurate and follows "the
trajectories" of the three philosophers' lives. There
is a fair amount of intellectual inquiry, but because
it examines Wittgenstein's actions as well as his
thoughts in a kind of "applied philosophy," the book
has a solid narrative quality about it, too. Moreover,
it's a perfect book if you're in a melancholy, reflective mood.

I discovered Wittgenstein when I was an undergraduate at Indiana University in the 1970s. To satisfy a "culture" requirement, I had landed over my head in a high-level philosophy class where we read, or in my case were supposed to read, works by Heidegger, Piaget, Freud, Bateson, Proust, Wittgenstein, and—get this—Carlos Castaneda.

Remember Castaneda and his Don Juan trilogy— *The Teachings of Don Juan: A Yaqui Way of Knowledge* (1969), *A Separate Reality: Further Conversations with Don Juan* (1971), and *Journey to Ixtlan: The Lessons of Don Juan* (1972)—which consists of the enigmatic ramblings of a Yaqui shaman as recorded by his peyote-eating sidekick? This trilogy was big on campus in the seventies, and it did a lot to increase illegal mushroom sales in the dormitories. Looking back, it's a little embarrassing to think that we held Castaneda in such reverential esteem, considering that I can recall nothing memorable in the narrator's hallucinatory accounts of getting blottoed.

As I said, this philosophy class, which met at the young professor's house and included refreshments of strong coffee and intestine-purging homemade apple cider, gave me my first exposure to Wittgenstein. Not that I fully understood him then or now, but at least Duffy's narrative about Wittgenstein's life has given me a framework within which I can begin to comprehend his philosophy. Wittgenstein spent many years away from the academic environment. He served in the Austrian army during World

War I and later taught in a remote mountain village. Perhaps because he had been born into a wealthy family, he shunned material possessions and lived ascetically most of his life, kind of like Castaneda's Don Juan, except he didn't eat a bunch of peyote buttons. Throughout his life, Wittgenstein did all he could to enrich his own spirituality and in later years made peace with himself.

Several scenes from this book have remained with me over the years: Wittgenstein flying his ten-foot-tall red dihedral kite off a cliff overlooking the Irish Sea (originally the philosopher wanted to be an aeronautical engineer), his horrific days in the Austrian army, and his stint as a schoolteacher in the town of Trattenbach, where the villagers found him odd and intimidating. Duffy writes that the inhabitants feared the wealth and intellect behind the schoolteacher's "aggressive" poverty. Although he was a humble man, Wittgenstein played this fear to his advantage. "Every St. Paul wants his Ephesians to know that he was formerly a Saul," writes Duffy.

If you're one of the fabled few who have read *The World As I Found It*, you might, out of respect for the author, bear with the only other book I know of by Duffy. *Last Comes the Egg* (1997) is the story of two troubled youths with family problems who grow up in Kennedy-era suburban Washington. But if you haven't read *World*, you should start looking for a copy for yourself, and then continue looking for copies for your thinking friends.

Ian Frazier: Close to the Midwest

Out of all the copies of Ian Frazier's *Dating Your Mom* (1986) that have rotated through my bookshelves, I have only one copy left of this collection of *New Yorker* pieces—and a fine copy it is. Rescued from the Hoopeston, Illinois, Public Library discard dolly, it has a thick plastic protective cover and a Dewey decimal classification number of 813.54, which I suspect is the designated category for books that defy community standards of wholesomeness and good taste.

I wonder if anyone from Hoopeston (the Sweet Corn Capital of the World and near my home-town of Milford, the Buckle on the Corn Belt) ever checked out Frazier's book and read the title essay about how young men struggling for intimacy with women might consider dating their own mothers (a relationship with "a grown, experienced woman"). Frazier's collection also includes "Kimberley Sol-zhenitsyn's Calendar," a spoof on the exiled Rus-sian writer Alexander Solzhenitsyn, which includes day calendar entries from their new life in the West: "May 10—Pick up the twins at band camp. Take Al's old Siberia clothes to Fire Dept. Rummage Sale." Admittedly, Frazier isn't the type of humor-ist that people in Hoopeston might find to their liking.

Dating Your Mom opened the door for me to other Frazier books, which are not necessarily humor-

ous, but which are exceptional works of nonfiction.*
Great Plains (1989) is a combination of travelogue
and history about this oft-forgotten region. If you
didn't know, I'm a big fan of the Midwest, which in
my personal geography stretches from the Allegh-
enies to the Rocky Mountains. Since Frazier writes
for the *New Yorker*, I was skeptical that he would
be sympathetic to his subject matter. Even though
I knew that Frazier had grown up in Ohio, I feared
he'd bash the Midwest, but I couldn't have been more
wrong. *Great Plains* is a truly masterful work, a perfect blend of history, travelogue, and personal quest.
Every time I reexamine the book I'm even more
impressed.

Rather than follow a preplanned route in *Great
Plains*, Frazier allows his curiosity and sense of
history and place to guide his travels. Driving
across Montana, North and South Dakota, western
Nebraska and Kansas, and West Texas in his rusted-
out van, he meanders through the history of the
prairie and wheat, the lore of the Old West. He talks
to gas station attendants, managers of cheap motels,
caretakers of one-room museums, and a missile silo

---

* Frazier's *Coyote v. Acme* (1996) is a similar set of humorous
essays. The title piece is a "legal document" in which Wile E.
Coyote, of Roadrunner cartoon fame, files a lawsuit against the
Acme Company for negligence in the manufacture of their products, which continually malfunction. In short, a description of all
those cartoons written in legalese. Worth picking up for that piece
alone.

tour guide, and becomes acquainted with several Native Americans.

One Oglala Sioux, Le War Lance, is first introduced in *Great Plains* and later becomes Frazier's guide in *On the Rez* (2000), a travelogue that concentrates on modern-day Native American life and culture on the Pine Ridge Reservation in South Dakota. Le War helps Frazier gain access to reservation life. Frazier manages to stay detached from his subjects (not trying to *be* Native American) while gaining the confidence of people on the reservation. He is neither apologetic nor judgmental about reservation life.

One noteworthy part of both *Plains* and *Rez* is Frazier's respect for the Sioux leader Crazy Horse. He goes to lengths to explain the spirituality of the great warrior. In *Great Plains*, Frazier takes us to the Crazy Horse Memorial near Mount Rushmore, which is still being blasted out of the rock by descendants of the sculptor Korczak Ziolkowski. Frazier points out that the sculpture is actually a ruin in reverse. "Instead of looking at it and imagining what it used to be," writes Frazier, "people stand at the observation deck and say, 'Boy, that's really going to be great someday.'"

Gabriel García Márquez: In Love

Fortunately for patrons of *The Book Shopper*, the supply-and-demand marketplace oftentimes has no respect for literature, even if you are a 1982 Nobel Prize winner and have received kudos from the rarefied Thomas Pynchon. Such is the case of the Latin American writer Gabriel García Márquez, whose books are readily available used or remaindered. Like many, I was introduced to Márquez (unaware at the time that his last name was actually García Márquez) through the surrealistic *One Hundred Years of Solitude* (1967), the century-long history of a family living in the strange, doomed village of Macondo. I still remember the girl who ate mouthfuls of earth whenever she was stressed and the year it rained every day, but the most memorable aspect of the book is the enchanting tone of García Márquez's narrative. I should reread it sometime to determine whether my memory is skewed because I consumed the book during my college years. I'm confident that it is still a fine book, but García Márquez's masterpiece is *Love in the Time of Cholera* (1988), which has the same surrealistic tone and sense of distant place as *Solitude* but has a more straightforward narrative.

Leaving aside romance novelists, whose books feature buff, wealthy couples (did they meet at the gym or in the waiting room at the plastic surgeon's office?), most "serious" contemporary novelists treat love as an exercise in pain or irresolvable conflict. Marriage is slavery, and love is nothing but a mixture of primordial urges and social climbing. No doubt there are some truths in these stories, but García Márquez reminds us that love can make us feel like conquistadors.

Love in the Time of Cholera is a book filled with longing and romance. García Márquez has reinvig-

Other García Márquez Bargains

Strange Pilgrims (1993) is a collection of García Márquez's short stories that has the cohesiveness of a novel. The author explains in the Prologue of the book how this unity came about. Over a period of eighteen years, he collected sixty-four story ideas in a notebook that "shipwrecked in a squall of papers" on his desk and was lost, never to be found. García Márquez attempted to re-create the story ideas—those he couldn't recall weren't, he figured, worth remembering.

Every story in *Strange Pilgrims* has the same basic premise: "the strange things that happen to Latin Americans in Europe." For example, in "I Only Came to Use the Phone," a young Mexican woman is stranded when her car breaks down near Barcelona. She catches a ride on a bus, but fails to realize that the bus is transporting women to a mental facility.

In *Chronicle of a Death Foretold* (1982), a very short novel, García Márquez employs an unusual plot device, revealing the deathly climax in the opening pages and then explaining the events leading up to the murder. *Living to Tell the Tale* (2003), the first volume of García Márquez's proposed

orated the sullied love story genre by creating the character of the not particularly handsome Florentino Ariza. ("He is ugly and sad, but he is all love.") Florentino's only true love is the beautiful Fermina Daza, who at first returns his affections but then three-volume autobiography, contains an account of a similar death. *Cholera* is based on the author's own parents' romantic beginnings, and the girl who eats mouthfuls of earth in *Solitude* is actually his sister Margot, the sibling with the "large, hallucinatory" eyes.

As you would expect, there is much magical realism in García Márquez's life, and his books seem to be an extension of his experiences. He has a passion for love, sex, and the senses—also for book shopping. In *Living to Tell the Tale*, he stumbles across remaindered copies of his own *Leaf Storm and Other Stories* (1979) for a peso a piece. "I bought all I could carry," he writes. This is good advice for all who have yet to read him.

suddenly rejects him and marries a doctor. Florentino is devastated but unbowed, and for the next fifty years he remains faithful to Fermina—which is not the same as chaste.

García Márquez tells stories and anecdotes about Florentino's wandering poetic soul and his peccadilloes with Fermina substitutes. These stories include such unforgettable quips as Florentino's observation that a man's penis "is like a firstborn son: you spend your life working with him, sacrificing everything for him, and at the moment of truth he does just as he pleases." *Cholera* also portrays late nineteenth- and early twentieth-century life in South America as a magical civilization similar to that of *Solitude*. Disease, pestilence, and sorrow exist, but it is also a world rich in tastes, smells, and touches.

In the final chapter, Florentino and Fermina take a river voyage together after a half century of separation. I wasn't the only one affected by this celebration of old love. The enigmatic Thomas Pynchon refers to the final chapter as "astonishing and symphonic." It's not an easy thing to describe love without being sappy, whether it is the love one has for another person or the love one has for a book.

Jim Harrison: Praiseworthy

Jim Harrison suffers from two image problems. Like another top writer, Richard Ford, he has a name that is too generic. I doubt whether Harrison and Ford (don't say them together too fast) care, since they are more interested in chronicling contemporary American life than in worrying about whether they are household names. When I want to explain quickly who Jim Harrison is, I say, "He's the author of the movie *Legends of the Fall*. You know, the movie starring Brad Pitt [I pause here to allow my female friends a moment to sigh] and Aidan Quinn. It's a film about two brothers who are in love with the same woman, and a father [Anthony Hopkins] who didn't teach the boys to share." But then I quickly add that the movie is based on one of three novellas in the book of the same name (1979)—one of the more than twenty books, including several volumes of poetry, that Harrison has penned.

Several of Harrison's books, *Dalva* (1988), the three novellas in *Julip* (1994), and *The Road Home* (1998), are as insightful and entertaining as anything I've read in my middle-age years. His autobiography, *Off to the Side: A Memoir* (2003), isn't a bad book either, as long as you can tolerate reading about people who live more robustly than you do. This is a reservation related to Harrison's second image problem, namely, that he is too much of a macho writer like Ernest Hemingway.

There are similarities between "Papa" and Harrison. They look alike—except Harrison has a more untamed appearance—they both spent considerable time in Michigan, and they both utilize a simple sentence style with a confident, matter-of-fact tone. One difference is that Hemingway is known for his "manly man" characters, whereas Harrison's men are equally tough but much better rounded. Yes, Harrison's middle-aged guys hunt, fish, and like dogs, but they aren't above pointing out their own foibles. A Harrison male appreciates birds and animals (instead of always wanting to blast them), and likes wine, food (Harrison has written a cookbook, *The Raw and the Cooked* [2001]), and strong women.

Among Harrison's strong female characters is the resourceful twenty-one-year-old Julip Durham in *Julip*, who has to get her mentally ill brother Bobby out of a Florida jail and into an institution. Then there is Dalva, the main character of the novel of the same name, who is a complex, free-spirited woman. She loves the natural world, "the sound of horses eating oats," "floating naked in the Niobrara [River] current on a hot afternoon in August," and the "strange looks of animals making love." Nevertheless, she struggles in her relationships with men throughout her life. In the novel, Dalva goes in search of the son she gave up for adoption when she became pregnant at age fifteen.

Dalva is also one of the narrators in *The Road Home*, a novel that covers three generations of a Nebraska family. This book unflinchingly tackles life's major conflicts: whom we love, how we decide to live, the role family history plays in our personalities, and how we face death. The problem some people may have with *The Road Home* is that there is no real plot. The narrative meanders like a flat, prairie river, and you must trust that Harrison, your guide, is taking you somewhere important. As a plot substitute, you get the wisdom and astute observations of Harrison's main characters. They live every moment to the fullest and refuse to mortgage their lives for profit or security.

Harrison has created the orneriest cuss in modern literature, in the middle-aged Black Dog, an indefatigable Native American who lives in the Upper Peninsula, drifting between menial jobs but smart enough, for example, to trade a female anthropologist information on ancestral burial grounds for a roll in the sack and a few hundred dollars. Harrison sees Black Dog's credo as "born not to cooperate with the world."

Black Dog first appears in *The Woman Lit by Fireflies* (1990), but Harrison brings him back several times, including in the novella *Westward Ho* in *The Beast God Forgot to Invent* (2000), where Black Dog is thrown out of his natural habitat into the phony world of Hollywood. He manages to adapt to the situation, and if that means breaking into the UCLA Botanical Gardens so he can camp out for the night, then so be it. Still not tired of Black Dog, Harrison makes him the protagonist of the title novella of *The Summer He Didn't Die* (2005). In this story Black Dog trades sex with a female dentist (she's "shaped like an egg") for a tooth extraction, and then rescues from permanent institutionalization a nature-loving child who suffers the aftereffects of fetal alcohol syndrome. Black Dog is a great character.

I've had some success finding used hardbacks to replace my paperback copies of Harrison's books and have often paid full price for new copies as gifts to friends—and myself. When I'm in a rut, I turn to Harrison. Since he celebrates the ordinary, the natural, and the mystery of our daily lives, he gives me some perspective on my own situation, which helps lift me out of my personal funk.

Oscar Hijuelos: Cuban Icon

Until I started reading Oscar Hijuelos, my exposure to the Cuban immigrant experience in America was limited to watching Desi Arnaz as Ricky Ricardo in the *I Love Lucy* television series. Whenever I watch those old black-and-white reruns of Ricky, Lucy, Fred, and Ethel, I focus on the flamboyant yet respectable and good-natured Ricky, with his full head of coal-black hair glued in place (which explains the hilarity if his hair ever got mussed). Ricky was a handsome and dashing, if unrealistic, example of the perfect immigrant, assimilating a new culture while respecting the homeland of his youth. Even if Lucy was merciless in her ribbing of Ricky's "hot-blooded" personality (like *she* was a sea of tranquility!) and Spanish accent, her barbs rolled effortlessly off Ricky's broad shoulder pads.

Lucy and Ricky make cameo appearances in Hijuelos's *The Mambo Kings Play Songs of Love* (1989), but there is more to the Cuban immigrant life than nights at the Copacabana and wondering what stunt that crazy redhead Lucy will pull next. Most immigrants, of course, become stuck to the burnt bottom of the melting pot—and often are more reviled than beloved.

Mambo Kings centers on two brothers, Cesar and Nestor Castillo, who emigrate from Cuba to New York City in 1949. Both are musicians—Cesar is a large, loud man and a boisterous singer, while the taciturn Nestor is a trumpet player and a quiet balladeer. (Isn't that just like siblings? Covering the emotional territory.) Their band, the Mambo Kings, achieves a moderate amount of success during the golden era of mambo. They even land a guest spot on *I Love Lucy*.

What makes this book exceptional is Hijuelos's ability to take the reader into a sensual world of music, passionate love and sex, and rich, exotic foods. (I developed a yearning for fried plantains.) Your tour guide is the boastful and gregarious Cesar, who regularly beds exotic women, such as the singers Vanna Vane and Dahlia Munez, the Argentine Flame of Passion.

Mambo Kings still has a powerful resonance with me. I can't watch a rerun of *I Love Lucy* without hoping to see Nestor and Cesar making a guest appearance. But even if Nestor and Cesar are no-shows, I'm not disappointed in the old sitcom, because there's always Ricky Ricardo, a man (or character) who remained emotionally true to his roots and culture with a dash of humor and style instead of anger or self-pity.

Another good book by Hijuelos is *Mr. Ives' Christmas* (1995), which I received as a gift. In this novel, Edward Ives, a commercial artist, grows up in New York City and is leading a respectable, spiritual life of good deeds when his son is tragically slain. Thereafter, Ives must cope with chronic depression and his doubts about faith and spirituality. Rounding out the plot are the sights and descriptions of the stoops and sidewalks of Ives's upper Manhattan neighborhood, populated with his circle of sensuous, robust friends.*

The only other book by Hijuelos that I can recommend is *Empress of the Splendid Season* (1999), the

---

* For more about *Mr. Ives' Christmas,* see Chapter 9, "Big Social Book Shopping Novels."

story of Cuban immigrant Lydia España, who lands in postwar New York. As she scrubs the homes of the wealthy she dreams of the life she wants and thinks she deserves—a life of comfort and beauty. Nevertheless she doesn't shirk her responsibilities and devotes herself to the raising of her two children. Conversely, never read *A Simple Habana Melody* (2000), the story of a rotund Cuban composer who eventually ends up in a concentration camp. (Hijuelos writes and writes and writes about the guy's girth and his adventurous, whopper of a penis.)

Mary Karr: Defining Families

> *A dysfunctional family is any family with more than one person in it.* —Mary Karr

Over lunch, a friend and I were discussing our family situations. We finally decided that every family has some type of issue—the wacky uncle who never holds a job, the substance-abusing cousin, the wayward daughter, son, or father. The number and degree of the situations may vary, but my friend summarized it best when he said, "Every family has its dysfunctional member. If you don't think so, you're probably it."

This bit of wisdom can be a long time in coming, because as you grow up in a family—any family—you may believe that your home life is the normal one and everyone else's family life is bizarre or fraught with problems. Then at some point—when you're visiting a family member in the mental ward of a hospital or the police have added your address to their patrol route—you realize that your family is starting to unravel. You could call it an "unfortunate situation," but that's much too sanitized a term for what has become a lousy, gut-wrenching, embarrassing, ever-present, major pain in the ass. How else could you describe being stuck caring for a person whom you'd love to cut loose from your life (despite the layer of guilt for feeling this way)? In these situations, very little can be done to make you feel better except to realize that almost everyone has a family meltdown problem that can be overcome (or at least won't last forever) and to listen to the story of someone who is in a far worse situation than yours.

Reading Mary Karr's memoirs, *The Liars' Club* (1995) and *Cherry* (2000), accounts of her years growing up in a sweaty, smelly East Texas oil town in the early 1960s, can be such a balm. One is amazed that not only did Karr survive her spectacularly dysfunctional family, but she wrote two fine books about it.

The trouble begins with Karr's mother, a frustrated artist who lacked nurturing instincts, or at least the temperament to be a parent. She also drank heavily, exacerbating the problem. She married seven times, including twice to Karr's father, a foreman at an oil refinery who would disappear for days because of work, extramarital affairs, or his own drinking sprees. I still remember the passages describing the time her unstable mother gathered up all the family belongings and burned them in the yard, and the way the family would eat their meals on the parents' huge bed. "We faced opposite walls, our backs together, looking like some four-headed totem," writes Karr, "our plates balanced on the spot of quilt between our legs. Mother called it picnic-style, but since I've been grown, I recall it as just plain odd."

Neither this book nor *Cherry*, which begins with Karr's puberty and goes through her high-school days, is bitter or completely dark. Karr has a detached, matter-of-fact type of comic tone that implies, "Isn't this the way all families are?"

Perhaps because she trained as a poet (she has published several collections), Karr is able to mix a richness of language with everyday vernacular. On C-SPAN, I once heard Karr read a passage from *Cherry*, about her first kiss, to an audience in Minnesota. She has a deadpan delivery, as if to keep from being too consumed by her memories. Understatement can be a powerful device when the experiences you are writing about are deep and painful as well as exhilarating. After the reading, Karr interjected jokes about the thousands of dollars she had spent on therapy to try to understand her messy early life. She is like the comedian with the bad childhood—tragedy underlies her jokes. It's a tribute to her and the power of her art that she has taken such experiences and molded them into a compelling and humorous story about how human beings can cope with just about anything.

Ultimately, every family may be a little wacky from time to time, but before you can accept the foibles and strengths of your own family, it helps to know that there's always someone who has it tougher. In the case of Mary Karr, that someone has survived to tell a fascinating and deeply moving story.

Maxine Hong Kingston: The Chinese-American Experience, Uncensored

Sure, China is always on our minds now—economic juggernaut, the 2008 Summer Olympics, and the hemorrhage of Jackie Chan movies, but it hasn't always been like that. Before Amy Tan of *The Joy Luck Club* (not to be confused with Mary Karr's *The Liars' Club*), there was the intelligent, reserved, and occasionally bawdy Maxine Hong Kingston.* Not only did her books help establish the genre of Chinese-American literature, but her omnipresence in used bookstores is second to none. Even Goodwill stores have copies of *The Woman Warrior* (1976) and *China Men* (1980). Although her books give us glimpses into the Chinese experience, what makes her more universally appealing is the way she understands the nature of alienation, the pressures to assimilate, and the shortcomings and strengths of different cultures. All that aside, what I like best about her writing is its subtle edge.

---

* Coincidentally, Mary Karr says Maxine Hong Kingston was a major influence on how to write a memoir.

China Men is a series of stories primarily about Chinese men who have immigrated to the United States. Kingston takes you inside the head of the Chinese immigrant—who was little better than a slave—building railroads through the Sierra Nevada mountains, working on sugar plantations in Hawaii, all the while cursing the white demons. A memorable scene in *China Men* is the visit of female missionaries to some Chinese laborers who agree to meet with the "Jesus demonesses" so they won't have to work in the sugar cane fields. Perhaps I remember this passage so well because I find the whole concept of missionaries troubling. Besides, a missionary's message isn't necessarily interpreted as it is intended. In the passage from *China Men*, the missionaries give the sugar cane workers presents that include pictures of the Crucifixion, but the laborers think the "grisly cards with a demon nailed to a cross" are a warning of what happens if you don't convert.

The Woman Warrior focuses on ghosts, spirits, and mystical fables, which reminds me of Carlos Castaneda's books—and you know how uneasy I feel about Castaneda. Besides, *China Men* has a more historical flavor, which I prefer. I didn't finish *Woman Warrior* my second time through, perhaps because the focal point of the book (Kingston's childhood) doesn't resonate with me.

I didn't finish reading Kingston's full-length novel, *Tripmaster Monkey: His Fake Book* (1987), either, but it will be worth another attempt in the future. (It's not unusual for me to give a book a second chance.)

Tripmaster is the story of the free-spirited Chinese-American Whitman Ah Sing, who hangs out in San Francisco during the turbulent 1960s. It's a tough read because Kingston likes to write long, Pynchon-esque paragraphs replete with free-association riffs using a wide variety of cultural (including pop) references. When I was familiar with the movie, play, or situation she referred to, I could get on her wavelength. Other times I got lost and had to jump on board again a few pages later.

Like the sixties "tour guides" who used to stay straight while others dropped acid, our *Tripmaster* tour guide is Whitman, who's irreverent, observant, and constantly rebelling against the mainstream. One example of how off-the-wall Kingston can be comes early in the book. As Whitman walks off his job as a toy department management trainee, he hikes up the wedding dress on a Bridal Barbie and sets an organ-grinder monkey with a red fez atop her. "Her legs held it hopping in place and clapping her with its cymbals. Her eyes opened and shut as the monkey bumped away at her."

Whitman Ah Sing reappears in Kingston's *The Fifth Book of Peace* (2003). *Peace* is a difficult book to describe because it is divided into four distinct parts:

- *Fire:* Kingston's account of losing her original manuscript in a 1991 fire on the day of her father's funeral.
- *Paper:* A history of the mythical Books of Peace.
- *Water:* In which Ah Sing takes his family to Hawaii in 1969 and becomes engaged in the anti-war

movement while trying to find peaceful harmony with his wife and young son.

- *Earth:* In which Kingston works with Vietnam veterans, helping them to write about their experiences in order to heal.

The irony is that to write a Book of Peace requires the telling of gruesome tales by the men and women who were in Vietnam. With all these themes and plot lines, the book reads a little disconnectedly. Still, Kingston is a "way show-er"—in the words of one writer-veteran—who charts a way out of the abyss of war. This toughness is one characteristic that sets Kingston apart. Not only is she a writer of elegant prose and a protector of Chinese heritage, but she also has some bite.

Milan Kundera: The Planet of Inexperience

Born in Czechoslovakia, Milan Kundera was forced into exile in France in 1975 because his writings were too unsettling for the ruling Communist government. His novels, stories, and essays address such topics as the relationships between men and women, how totalitarian governments obliterate lives, and the nature of art and storytelling.

Kundera has a strong hold on me for several reasons. *Life Is Elsewhere* (1974), the story of a struggling poet who, according to the narrator, was "uninterestingly odd rather than oddly interesting," was one of the first remaindered books I ever purchased. I saw it in a mall bookstore in 1976 and remembered that it had been reviewed in *Time* magazine. I couldn't recall anything about the review except Kundera's picture. The strong Czech expatriate looked Scandinavian, but even more memorable was his intense, glaring, writer's scowl. He writes with a scowl, too.

Since the book was so inexpensive, I was willing to take a chance, and I went on to read a number of Kundera's books. This anecdote illustrates one of the bonuses of book shopping: it encourages you to gamble on a writer you are not sure about. You have to pay with your time, but not with your money.

I have usually picked up Kundera's books as remainders within a year or two of publication, and I've devoted a significant portion of my limited bookshelf space to him. My selection includes his collection of short stories, *Laughable Loves* (1974), *The Book of Laughter and Forgetting* (1980), a novel that resulted in his Czech citizenship being revoked, *The Unbearable Lightness of Being* (1984), a novel about love and marriage intertwined with political overtones, and the novel *Immortality* (1991). Another book, *Slowness* (1996), is a very short novella that juxtaposes two events: an intensely romantic eighteenth-century night of seduction at a château near Paris and a harried late-twentieth-century one-night stand at the same château. *Slowness* was advertised as Kundera's "most humorous book yet." This may be true, but on the funny spectrum, I rank Kundera right next to Alexander Solzhenitsyn.

Kundera is an admirable writer because he never takes the safe party line. ("Union of Soviet Socialist Republics: 'Four words, four lies.'")* He has a different perspective on events and doesn't mind letting you know about it.

I'm not the only person who thinks Kundera is a literary heavyweight with a striking appearance. Philip Roth's novel *The Human Stain* (2000) pays homage to Kundera through one of the characters, a classics professor named Delphine. In the book, she attends a lecture given by Kundera in Paris. She loves "his Eastern Europeanness," his restless intellectual nature, and his "poetically prizefighterish looks."

Sometimes, however, Kundera is just too much. I recently reread *Unbearable Lightness* and struggled to stay interested in the self-absorbed main characters. Even the incessant lovemaking, or a female character prancing naked over a mirror, couldn't overcome the overwrought tone of this book.† I was embarrassed to think I had liked it so much. I must keep reminding myself to exercise caution before recommending a book I haven't read since I was thirty years old.

---

* From Kundera's essay "Sixty-three Words," in *The Art of the Novel* (1988).

† In the late 1980s, Philip Kaufman directed a film version of *The Unbearable Lightness of Being* starring Daniel Day-Lewis, Lena Olin, and Juliette Binoche. I found the movie—for lack of a better word —unbearable. Again, the characters seemed too self-absorbed for me to like them.

But I am able to forgive myself, since according to Kundera we live on the Planet of Inexperience. Inexperience is "a quality of the human condition," he writes. "We are born one time only, we can never start a new life equipped with the experience we've gained from a previous one. We leave childhood without knowing what youth is, we marry without knowing what it is to be married, and even when we enter old age, we don't know what it is we're heading for: the old are innocent children of their own age. In that sense, man's world is the planet of inexperience."*

Alice McDermott: Young Love, Crazy Love

Alice McDermott's *That Night* (1987) is a book that continues to impress. *New York Times* critic Michiko Kakutani referred to the book in her 2002 review of Alice Sebold's acclaimed *The Lovely Bones*: "The novel is an elegy," wrote Kakutani, "much like Alice McDermott's *That Night*, about a vanished place and time and the loss of childhood innocence."

That Night is the story of young high-school love —impassioned, reckless, the kind that creates madness in parents. Setting her novel in the early 1960s in suburban Long Island, McDermott writes about the lonely void of suburbia. Maybe that's why the love affair between the two main characters, Sheryl and Rick, seems so steamy and alive.

* From "Sixty-three Words," in *The Art of the Novel*.

I'll always remember the opening scene where Rick comes to pick up his girlfriend, Sheryl, only to discover that Sheryl's mother has sent her away. In a haunting and morose tone, the book's narrator, a young girl who also lives in the neighborhood, describes Rick: "he stood on the short lawn before her house, his knees bent, his fists driven into his thighs, and bellowed her name with such passion . . . he cried 'Sherry,' drawing out the word, keening it, his voice both strong and desperate." (Yes, kind of like Marlon Brando wailing for Stella, but fortunately McDermott doesn't write that.)*

I've read a paperback copy of McDermott's first novel, *A Bigamist's Daughter* (1982), which has more or less the same tone as *That Night*. The narrator is a woman who recruits writers for a vanity press. She preys on the hopes and expectations of would-be authors—a path of certain disappointment for her clients.

Based on having read those two books, I picked up a copy of *At Weddings and Wakes* (1992), which I found as a public library discard on a bookstore discount table. Despite two attempts to read through this short novel, I couldn't force myself to be interested in *Weddings*. Several orphaned children are raised by relatives in suburban Long Island in the 1960s. The extended Irish-Catholic family has all

---

* Hollywood made a movie titled *That Night* starring Juliette Lewis, and I am curious to see it, but it is only available on VHS.

kinds of subtle problems and secrets, but McDer-mott purposely avoids using proper names and the timeline skips around, all of which make the book a little too subtle for my taste.

Since my McDermott impasse, she has written quite a few more books, including *Charming Billy* (1998), which won the National Book Award, *Child of My Heart* (2003), and *After This* (2007). This grow-ing recognition of her work benefits the book shop-per, as more copies of her work eventually become available at fine used bookstores everywhere.

E. Annie Proulx: Acceptance

Annie Proulx's career took off when her book *Post-cards* (1992) received critical acclaim and her fol-low-up novel, *The Shipping News* (1993), won the Pulitzer for fiction. *Shipping News* is about a likable but thick-in-the-waist-and-mind character named Quoyle, who after the death of his wife moves to a remote part of Newfoundland with his two daugh-ters and aunt to try to reclaim his life. Quoyle works for a bizarre local newspaper called the *Gammy Bird*, a yellow-journal scandal sheet whose credo is that if it publishes enough wrecked car photos and sexual abuse stories people will read it. In this raw, cold environment, Quoyle eventually learns to accept himself and discovers love without pain or misery. (Read more about Proulx in Chapter 9, "Big Social Book Shopping Novels.")

A similar novel is Proulx's *That Old Ace in the Hole* (2002), in which Bob Dollar, an impressionable young man (desperately in need of a job) is sent on a secret mission in the Texas panhandle to scout out potential locations for a cruel and foul-smelling hog farm. As in *The Shipping News*, Proulx introduces a host of small-town characters whom she treats with humor and sympathy. This generosity is one of Proulx's strengths as a writer, in contrast to Carolyn Chute, who is relentlessly depressing in her depiction of those less fortunate.*

In general, Proulx's work focuses on people who live their lives without safety nets and have finally fallen too far to get up. While they have learned a lot about gardening, hunting, and living with nature, they also bear scars from tainted family histories that influence and sour each new relationship. Proulx has a bone-chilling sense of the hardscrabble life, which can be attributed in part to her days as a small-town journalist. She spent years writing in obscurity (like most of us) and learned her craft in the minors by producing freelance articles on a variety of subjects, including nature, agriculture, and architecture.

---

* Chute is the author of several books, including *The Beans of Egypt, Maine* (1985) and the more recent *The School on Heart's Content Road* (2008). I've read *Beans* and I can see why she gets acclamation for chronicling the plight of the poor, but she spares no stinking detail about the filthy, intermarrying, hard-drinking, ever-procreating life of her characters, and that can be overwhelming.

An understanding of Proulx's writing life and style came from a book shopper friend of mine (another former journalist, no less) who showed me a copy of a nonfiction book by Proulx. It was a gardening book about how to build backyard construction projects such as trellises and brick patios—nothing extraordinary, per se, but you can appreciate where Proulx honed her writing skills and developed her gutsy forbearance. During her years as a journalist, she learned to write in clear, precise language. Moreover, her long apprenticeship deepened her understanding of the role of patience in not only her own life, but the lives of her characters as well.

So there is my list of used bookstore standard bearers. No self-respecting used bookstore should be without a majority of these writers. When I do a "pass-in-review" (a military term for a commander surveying his troops), I expect to see enough books by these authors to put me at ease and motivate me to keep looking. I don't keep score or have a rating system beyond that. For me, what ultimately defines a good bookstore is my willingness to drop a wad of money. I'm a guy with a paucity of shelf space and a backlog of reading. When I'm in a place that tugs at my wallet and tempts me with more literary riches than I can carry home, I know I will return.

More Proulx

Though Annie Proulx's books aren't difficult to find, be warned that she can be a downer to read. *Accordion Crimes* (1996) is a predictable book that tells the history of a little green accordion and the series of depressed people (economically and emotionally) who own it. Manufactured in Sicily near the turn of the twentieth century, the accordion enters the U.S. at the port of New Orleans. The little squeezebox with the hoarse, groaning sound travels around the country "reminding listeners of the brutalities of love, of various hungers."

If that's not depressing enough, check out "Brokeback Mountain," from her short story collection, *Close Range: Wyoming Stories* (1999). "Brokeback Mountain" is the sad tale of two lonely ranch hands who discover and wrestle with their alternative cowboy lifestyles while watching sheep on the wide-open range. As those familiar with the movie know, it doesn't end well for the two men. (See also Chapter 11 on Larry McMurtry.)

Depressing or not, *Postcards* is one of my favorites. It's the saga of the Blood family, who owns a small dairy farm in Vermont. The Bloods have three children, Loyal, the one-armed Dub, and a daughter, Mernelle. In the opening pages, Loyal murders his girlfriend and leaves the family, who cannot survive without its able-bodied oldest son. As punishment for his transgression, Loyal spends his entire long life as a drifter. I am not sure what the other family members did to deserve their ill fates, but with Proulx some of the problems the working poor face are the result of forces beyond their control. Despite the bleak premise, the book has many delightful passages where the author tweaks those who are better off but have little common sense.

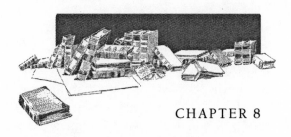

Growing Old with the New Journalists

MY RELATIONSHIP WITH New Journalist Ray Mungo dates back to my undergraduate days, when I picked up a paperback copy of his *Famous Long Ago: My Life and Hard Times with Liberation News Service* (1970) for a quarter at an Indiana University Library used book sale. The professor in my Introduction to Journalism class had mentioned the book in a lecture, and the unusual title must have stuck in my mind. This was probably 1973 or 1974, a time when there seemed to be a misty cloud of disappointment hovering over campuses that we had missed out on the romantic chaos of the sixties. We did have to register for the draft, but the war was over except for the cinematic fall of Saigon, which we watched on the news in our dorm rooms. We knew that the blah seventies were nothing like the turbulent sixties, except for the abundance of marijuana.

In my senior year, a professor offered a seminar called New Journalism, which included the works of Norman Mailer, Truman Capote, Hunter S. Thompson, Joan Didion, and Tom Wolfe. New Journalism is not a term you hear much any more, but back then it was considered a form of reporting that was anointed as being "more truthful" than what you read in the newspaper. Journalism is supposed to be objective, but the premise is suspect, because of the hidden bias in, for example, how an article is placed on the page, which details are edited out, and whether the headline correctly matches the article's content. These changes are invisible to the reader, many of whom still think that if it's in print, it's true. Not necessarily.

During the sixties, all major institutions were re-evaluated and journalism was no exception. Critics raised questions about the meaning of objectivity and truth. When the New Journalists came along, they reported events, but readily admitted and recorded their own reactions to them. They showed their readers their personal biases, and they brought their own personalities or created personalities to view the events. Ray Mungo was the happy hippie and Hunter S. Thompson the macho, hard-living paranoiac. Didion was the dry and detached intellectual, and Wolfe was the cool hipster. They became characters in their own articles and books, and to a degree, readers had to accept the author's personality and bias to believe the stories they were reading.

You can see their influence in feature stories today, since it is not uncommon for current writers to focus on themselves more than on the subject they are writing about. Because of this, New Journalism's ideas seem passé now, but in the late sixties and early seventies, they were considered ground-breaking. I will defer to scholars on the historical significance of the New Journalists, but what impresses me most is that these counterculture writers who were introduced to me in the early seventies are still (with the exception of Mungo) making regular appearances on the mainstream bestseller lists. Tom Wolfe's latest novels, *A Man in Full* (1998) and *I Am Charlotte Simmons* (2004), were huge bestsellers, and Joan Didion's book about the loss of her husband, *The Year of Magical Thinking* (2005), has sold 200,000 copies.

Mungo's Works

Famous Long Ago is Ray Mungo's personal account of the rise and fall of the alternative press, which arose out of opposition to the Vietnam War. It was written almost immediately after those tumultuous times and thus avoids the major pitfall of most reminiscences about the period: "If you remember the sixties, you probably weren't there." Mungo was there, as the editor of the Liberation News Service, an alternative, antiwar news network that wasn't a slave to the established media of the day. Mungo sets the tone with the opening paragraph, which you may recognize from the first chapter of *The Book Shopper.*

> What follows is a story, by no means complete, of what happened to me during the few years after I started. Please don't try to learn anything from it, for there is

no message. Try to enjoy it, as I have (at least much of the time) enjoyed putting it down for you. Take it slow, don't try to read it in one sitting, by all means get distracted from time to time. Read it stoned, read it straight, give up and never finish it, it's all the same between friends. Take care of your health and get plenty of rest.

Following *Famous Long Ago* were two more hippie books, one about his farm in Vermont, the other about a trip to Japan. The three were packaged into a trilogy called *Mungobus* (1979). Mungo is also a baseball fan. He wrote about his big league travels in *Confessions from Left Field: A Baseball Pilgrimage* (1983), but surprisingly the book *does not* include his best piece about baseball, "Confessions from Left Field." In that essay, Mungo recounts a dreary trip to Candlestick Park in San Francisco, where a Giants fan leans too far over the rail to abuse his team and accidentally falls to his death. Mungo writes, "You root for the home team and if they don't win it's a shame. But enough is enough."*

The Mungo book I continue to admire most is *Cosmic Profit: How to Make Money Without Doing Time* (1979). In this book, Mungo looks at alternative-style businesses that have incorporated sixties' ideals into successful enterprises. The entrepreneurs profiled have a different approach to work and their workers. Chapters describe businesses such as Celes-

---

* "Confessions from Left Field" does appear in the baseball anthology, *Writing Baseball* (1991), edited by Jerry Klinkowitz.

tial Seasonings in Colorado, a cannery in Northern California, and Mungo's own bookstore in Seattle. Throughout the book, Mungo provides examples of people who found their bliss doing what they loved and making enough money to support themselves and others. He has a great line somewhere in the book (and I've looked so much I'm beginning to doubt that it ever existed) that says, "If time is money, the unemployed are the richest people in the world." Mungo wrote thirty years ago that we use money to buy time, and that hasn't changed.

Throughout my spotty work life (I avoid the word "career," which would indicate some plan to my succession of jobs), I've experienced down times when I was laid off or had made a move for the sake of my ex-wife's job. During those hiatuses I found *Cosmic Profit* relevant and comforting. To keep from going into total panic mode, I would take advantage of the time off to do some local sightseeing or catch up on my reading and writing. I also dreamed up some cosmic profit jobs, like renting books on tape out of abandoned one-hour photo booths or setting up a store where people would come in and you'd write a story about their life for them (kind of like drawing a fifteen-minute portrait at the amusement park). In some ways, writing *The Book Shopper* has been a cosmic profit endeavor.

For the longest time, I wasn't really sure what had become of Ray Mungo. I asked about him when I was perusing some used bookstores in Seattle, but no one seemed to have heard of him. He had gone on to write books about buying houses with little or no money down, and books about Liberace, Palm Springs, and San Francisco, but nothing much in the last fifteen years. I figured he was "off-the-grid," but as I did a final fact-check for this book, I found that he has re-emerged on (where else?) the web, at raymondmungo.com. He looks happy; I'm not surprised.

Hunter S. Thompson

Hunter Thompson's influence on campus cannot be overstated. It rivaled the symphonic techno-rock of Yes's *Close to the Edge* and *The Dark Side of the Moon* posters as the dormitory icons of the age. A classmate of mine could recite verbatim the opening paragraph of Thompson's *Fear and Loathing in Las Vegas* (1972), which begins, "We were somewhere around Barstow on the edge of the desert when the drugs began to take hold." I'm proud to say that there was never a time I could recite the entire opening paragraph of *Fear and Loathing* by memory,* but I do occasionally peruse his gonzo style of journalism, as he called

---

* Years later, David Owen's opener in *The Walls Around Us: The Thinking Person's Guide to How a House Works* (1991) usurped Thompson's top ranking. It goes: "I love buying expensive power tools and using them to wreck various parts of my house." It proves how our priorities change when we grow older.

it, the drug-crazed prose that was characterized by rants of disrespect for any authority (police, politicians, editors). He always seems funny at first, but his persona quickly wears thin for me.

On the other hand, I still admire his first nonfiction book, *Hell's Angels: A Strange and Terrible Saga* (1966). In this tale, Thompson travels undercover with the Bay Area Angels and lives to write about it with detail and empathy. The book is void of all the gonzo megalomania that dominates the rest of his work, and it was republished as a Modern Library Classic in 1999. Thompson is better read in small doses, so I recommend the bargain-priced collection *The Great Shark Hunt: Strange Tales from a Strange Time* (1979), because it contains brief excerpts from *Fear and Loathing, Hell's Angels*, and his other works. *Great Shark* also has an article titled "What Lured Hemingway to Ketchum?" in which a perfectly rational Thompson (this was 1964) visits the Idaho town where Hemingway killed himself with a shotgun. It has lately become a more interesting read, in light of Thompson's own suicide by gunshot at his Colorado home in February 2005. In the Ketchum story, Thompson prophetically says that writers who lose their power of conviction lose the willingness to create art out of chaos. Ironically, this assessment applied to Thompson and his later works as well. When his personality was co-opted as the model for "Uncle" Duke in Garry Trudeau's *Doonesbury* comic strip—and later as a character in a couple of movies

—the real Thompson became overshadowed by the caricature.* Thompson the reporter had ceased to exist, but if you read *Hell's Angels* or excerpts from *The Great Shark Hunt*, you'll know that it wasn't always that way.

Joan Didion: Coping in the Sixties and Seventies

Like Hunter Thompson, Joan Didion has had troubles with aging. *The Year of Magical Thinking* is Didion's memoir of the devastating year following the sudden death of her longtime husband, the writer John Gregory Dunne, in December 2003—a year during which her daughter was seriously ill.† Given the subject matter, it surprises me that this book was a bestseller, and I suspect that many copies will be hitting the remainder market or used bookstores in the next few years. I've observed over time that this type of book is one that a lot of people believe "will do them good" or "be cathartic," but it is that category of demanding books which usually remains unread.

Like most people, I avoid painful subjects, but it *is* Joan Didion, a book shopper's stalwart, so I picked

---

* Bill Murray played Thompson in *Where the Buffalo Roam* (1980), and Johnny Depp played Raoul Duke in *Fear and Loathing in Las Vegas* (1998).

† *The Year of Magical Thinking* mostly chronicles Didion's loss of her husband. At the same time, her daughter, Quintana, was in and out of hospitals with infections that eventually claimed her life in August 2005, just a few months before the book was published.

up a pristine, secondhand paperback copy a few months ago. What a book! It is impressive because not only is the author able to reveal her most intimate thoughts—especially the things we tell ourselves in order to cope—but it is so insightful about the nature of grief. (The year of magical thinking is the year you think your loved one is coming back.) *Magical Thinking* deserves the same shelf life that her two best books still enjoy. Both are collections of essays, *Slouching Towards Bethlehem* (1968) and *The White Album* (1979).

If you care to learn about or relive the late sixties and seventies, these two books capture that era. Unlike Thompson with his drug-crazed paranoia, Didion steps back and synthesizes places and events with sparse clarity. In the title essay from *Bethlehem*, Didion, a patient nonparticipating observer, squats almost unnoticed in the living room of some "love children." Of course, these "love children" were runaways who thought of themselves as revolutionaries, but in reality they were just unhappy drug users trying to forget and escape. Didion was no lightweight with drugs herself. (In the preface to *Bethlehem* she enumerates her own list of preferred painkillers.) Throughout the long article, she reports in a steady, detached tone that builds in intensity to the final scene, where she captures the pathetic misery of the Haight-Ashbury district in San Francisco. Didion goes a long way toward debunking the myth of the sixties as the Age of Aquarius. Later she reinforces that view in the title article from *The White Album*, where she points to the bloody Manson murders as the end of the sixties.

I've read Didion's novels *Play It As It Lays* (1970) and *The Last Thing He Wanted* (1996), and I'm in agreement with Sarah Vowell, who wrote an analysis of her work in *The Salon.com Reader's Guide to Contemporary Authors*. Vowell says that reading Didion's fiction is "like looking at Le Corbusier furniture: It's pristine, beautiful, downright perfect, and yet not particularly inviting to live with—a little cold, a little cruel, a little too angular to accommodate human curves."

Tom Wolfe: The Early Sixties and More

I debated whether to put Tom Wolfe here with the New Journalists or with the social novelists in the next chapter, "Big Social Book Shopping Novels." The deciding factors were that Wolfe, though he has written about many things, has never tackled the intricacies of book shopping, and his journalistic endeavors far exceed his work as a novelist. That's not to disparage his novels, but some of his nonfiction work, particularly *The Right Stuff* (1979), is without equal. *The Right Stuff* is extraordinary in the way it captures the mood of the country in the late 1950s and early 1960s. Wolfe wrote it with such verve and showmanship that I have considered reading the whole book again.

Besides, Tom Wolfe is one of the founders of New Journalism. He introduced this style in 1963 with

the feature story about custom cars in *Esquire* entitled "There Goes (Varoom! Varoom!) That Kandy-
Kolored (Thphhhhhh!) Tangerine-Flake Streamline
Baby (Rahghhh!) Around the Bend (Brummmmmm-
mmmmmmmmmmmmm) . . . . . ." Wolfe then rode
with Ken Kesey and the Merry Pranksters and wrote
about it in *The Electric Kool-Aid Acid Test* (1968).
These titles alone give you a sense of his energy.

Wolfe's borderline zany prose style character-
izes all his writing, but it serves him best in *The
Right Stuff*, the story of the seven Mercury Astronauts (along with test pilot Chuck Yeager) and the
early days of the fledgling U.S. Space Program.
Wolfe draws detailed portraits of John Glenn, Alan
Shepard, and Gus Grissom, to name a few of the
pilots who thrived on their dangerous career paths
while their wives dreaded a visit from some "com-
petent long-faced figure . . . some Friend of Widows
and Orphans" who would regretfully inform them
their husbands were dead. He explains what the
Right Stuff is—the grit of those who had the cour-
age, skill, and devil-may-care attitude to be the top
test pilots, and later astronauts.

The men with the right stuff were a select few, and
Wolfe juxtaposes their unique experiences against
the backdrop of a nation that cheered their every
move on television and in the pages of *Life* magazine.
His customary use of zealous language is in sharp
contrast to the potentially dull setting. Don't forget
these times had an aura of innocence. But Wolfe's
wild descriptions of the mundane air force bases,

and his ability to cut through the technical space jargon with riffs of prose, add a whole level of excitement to the book. Although Wolfe would later lay claim to writing some great social novels like *Bonfire of the Vanities* (1987) and *A Man in Full*, I believe *The Right Stuff* is a far more compelling and creatively told story.

Perhaps Wolfe's real strength lies beyond his journalistic or novelistic skills. Wolfe's talents include a knack for encapsulating historical ideas and events into an understandable context. Known best for his labeling of the self-indulgent 1970s as the Me Decade, Wolfe put his powers of analysis to use in his slim treatise *From Bauhaus to Our House* (1981). In addition to being a flame on modern architecture, *Bauhaus* is a primer for people who want to know a little about twentieth-century architecture without a lot of suffering. Sure, you won't get all of Wolfe's inside jokes and digs, but you'll come away with enough to appreciate Sarah Vowell's joke about Joan Didion's fiction ("like looking at Le Corbusier furniture").

The same is true of Wolfe's collection *Hooking Up* (2000). The strongest piece isn't "My Three Stooges," his rebuttal to John Updike's, Norman Mailer's, and John Irving's contention that *A Man in Full* wasn't a praiseworthy novel, but rather the memorable "Two Young Men Who Went West," a thumbnail explanation of the origins of Silicon Valley. In this brief biography of Robert Noyce, one of the inventors of the integrated circuit and one of the founders of

Intel, Wolfe reveals the serendipitous nature of how the son of a Congregational minister with Iowa roots set the pace for Silicon Valley culture.

I'm not saying that Wolfe's fiction or journalism isn't good; it's just that when he combines his skills as novelist and reporter with his ability to synthesize history and ideas into highly entertaining prose, you recognize what sets him apart from other writers. Amazingly, Wolfe's best is readily available for next to nothing. I paid a dollar for my hardcover copy of *The Right Stuff*, and I found *Hooking Up* for three bucks at an antiques mall in Clinton, Tennessee.

In my view, the impact of the New Journalists is unparalleled. Three of the four writers I mentioned are practically household names—still. Try to think of another school of writers in the last half century that has had a stronger impact on style or covered a wider range of the topics they have covered in politics, social history, and current events.

The Book Shopper pays homage to the New Journalists because their technique of mixing their personal voices with their reportage provided a precedent that enabled me to mix my personal story with a history of contemporary literature. How much would I have lost out on if I hadn't been exposed to those writers at Indiana University? Although my upper-level seminar was taught by an eclectic, erudite professor, who lectured in obscure literary vocabulary that seemed like a foreign language to my corn-fed ears, I managed to remember a few useful tidbits. Not only did

Tom Wolfe as the Man in Full

I think the reason that Wolfe's bigger-than-life persona—his white suits, his witty prose, and his claim to being a social novelist of the magnitude of Charles Dickens—does not grate against my Midwestern sensibilities is that for the most part *A Man in Full* (1998) lives up to the hype that preceded it. This 742-page novel on the sprawling upscale New South is much better than *Bonfire*, which I didn't even bother finishing, and I found it more readable than *David Copperfield*. For all its heft, however, it lacks the soul of other social novels such as Richard Ford's *Independence Day* (1995) or Jonathan Franzen's *The Corrections* (2001).

Perhaps it's asking too much for a book that tackles corporate avarice and how it causes additional poverty and hardship to the already economically disadvantaged to be soulful as well. It's like expecting Oliver Stone's *Wall Street* to be an introspective flick, something like *My Dinner with Gecko*.

The main character in *A Man in Full* is sixty-year-old Charlie Coker, a former college football player now a real estate developer, whose decadent lifestyle (a 29,000-acre Georgia plantation used for raising horses, hunting quail, and impressing

I find out what was worth reading, but as a writer I learned that putting to paper your own reactions to events and experiences is acceptable, as long as you are honest with your readers and yourself.

clients) comes to a halt when his 40-story office-building development turns into a bust. Forced to make draconian economic cuts, he lays off workers all over his empire, including a struggling laborer, Conrad Hensley, who after being pink-slipped ends up in prison. Predictably, Coker and Hensley cross paths as the book progresses. There are some memorable sections, among them the chapter where Coker's creditors invite him for a come-to-Jesus financial "workout" and verbally beat him until saddlebags of sweat seep down his shirt. In another chapter, Wolfe spares no detail in describing equine lust at the plantation's breeding barn ("the stallion came crashing down on the mare's back and drove his enormous penis toward her yawning vulva"). Now that's literature!

I'm not sure if kids in the eighth grade will be reading Wolfe fifty years from now (I'm not sure they will be reading anything), but he writes page-turners with pulpy appeal. Students of the future, enjoy.

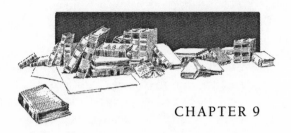

CHAPTER 9

Big Social Book Shopping Novels

AS THE SAYING GOES, when you're a hammer everything in life looks like a nail, and the same is true with reading when you're a book shopper. As I cruise control over the words on a page—believe me, I don't pore over the meaning of every sentence—I always tap on the brakes when I run across a passage about book shopping. I feel that it is one of those serendipitous moments when the author has put something in the book specifically for me. Several well-known authors have obliged. For example, I pulled out my highlighter when Oscar Hijuelos in *Mr. Ives' Christmas* (1995)* waxes poetic about the used books Mrs. Ives purchases for Pablo, the boyfriend of her daughter, Caroline:

> And because Pablo had always liked books and treated Caroline so well, and liked to show her the essays he wrote in school, she insisted upon buying him paper-

* See Chapter 7, "Prerequisites: What Every Good Used Bookstore Should Have."

back novels, five or six at a time, crumbling, moldy, second-hand inexpensive editions that hardly made a dent in her budget. How could she resist a twenty-five-cent edition of *Sons and Lovers*, *Dubliners*, *Bleak House*, *Moby Dick*, or for that matter, *Don Quixote* or *Sonnets of Shakespeare* for the same price as a slice of pizza?

I guess it figures that, out of that entire book, the line I specifically remember is the "slice of pizza" sentence. It's a comfort to know that some of our best modern writers appreciate the nuances of book shopping and have included snippets of this noble activity in their work.

Annie Proulx is another writer who knows the pleasures and pitfalls of book shopping. In "On the Antler," from her *Heart Songs and Other Stories* (1988), the main character, Hawkwheel—a man "in the insomnia of old age"—spends his days and nights crammed in his trailer, reading. He hasn't always been a reader, but lately he's developed an appreciation for classic nature books such as John Beever's *Practical Fly-Fishing*. He gets some real bargains by taking advantage of a local bully who is liquidating his grandfather's book collection until some helpful "liberian" from the state college butts in and ruins Hawkwheel's good thing, by telling the bully how much the collection is really worth. A distraught Hawkwheel goes berserk and tears up some of the fine books he already has. Hawkwheel fails to heed one of the axioms of book shopping—the real value of good books is in the reading.

Even more important, Proulx's impressive and decorated career may have hinged on the fortuitous nature of book shopping. In an acknowledgment of her Pulitzer Prize for *The Shipping News* (1993), Proulx refers to the influence of book shopping. "And without the inspiration of Clifford W. Ashley's wonderful 1944 work, *The Ashley Book of Knots*," she writes, "which I had the good fortune to find at a yard sale for a quarter, this book would have remained just the thread of an idea." Several chapters in *Shipping News* are named after knots, such as the Slippery Hitch or the Strangle Knot, which have a symbolic tie-in to the plot. The struggling main character, Quoyle, is described as someone "easily walked on," and the novel's plot centers on Quoyle's attempt to rise above his doormat personality. *The Ashley Book of Knots* is a fantastically realized metaphor for the novel—and it began with a yard sale.

Book shopping also makes cameo appearances in what I consider the two major social novels of our times, Jonathan Franzen's *The Corrections* (2001) and Richard Ford's *Independence Day* (1995).* When I think of social novels, I think of the Charles Dickens I had to read in high school and college. Even though they were tedious reading for me, I was still impressed that a story could unwittingly transport

* It's not easy talking about *Independence Day* without including Ford's subsequent novel, *The Lay of the Land* (2006), which is a continuation of *Independence Day*. I'm not sure you can read *The Lay of the Land* without reading *Independence Day* first.

me into nineteenth-century England. It was complete immersion that included lifestyles, language, the manners of courtship, economic uncertainties, and social calamities. Tromp through a Dickens novel (major speed reading required) and you can't help getting a sense of what life was like back then.

Jonathan Franzen, in his 2002 essay "Why Bother?" (a rewrite of his well-known 1996 essay, "Perchance to Dream," originally published in *Harper's*), mused compellingly about why one should bother writing novels, when television and movies so dominate the culture. He partially defined the social novel as a book that "must span private experiences in a public context." In other words, Franzen argued that the fictional characters must reflect what is happening in the wider society. Although he presented a persuasive argument that it is a nearly hopeless endeavor to write a social novel, he turned around and did it in *The Corrections*, which focuses on a normal, miserable, middle-class Midwestern family, the Lamberts, but broadens to include commentary about the whirlwind economic boom of the 1990s. Against the backdrop of relative prosperity, people were still psychologically impoverished, depressed, and struggling to connect to each other.

In *The Corrections*, Alfred and Enid Lambert and their grown children Chip, Denise, and Gary, all have problems that we can recognize. Alfred is losing his mental faculties because of Parkinson's disease, and Enid has the burden of being the solo round-the-clock caregiver. Though financially successful, Gary is clinically depressed, and his marriage is in trouble. (Franzen is chillingly accurate in his depiction of how married couples can emotionally manipulate each other.) The hardboiled Denise has trouble with her relationships with men, and Chip is a man-child who has difficulty controlling his sexual appetites, his spending, and his self-loathing. In one hilarious scene (good ol' black humor), the deluded and depleted Chip sinks so low that he resorts to shoplifting several pounds of Norwegian salmon by stuffing it into the crotch of his pants. ("The dangling filet felt like a cool, loaded diaper.")

In keeping with his mission to write a big social novel, Franzen includes reportage of one of the most booming economic eras of modern times, the dot.com frenzy of the late 1990s, which spilled over into other regions of the world, such as Lithuania. The ills of modernity are evident throughout the globe. The only difference between the free market economy of America and the black market of Lithuania "was that in America the wealthy few subdued the unwealthy many by means of mind-numbing and soul-killing entertainments and gadgetry and pharmaceuticals, whereas in Lithuania, the powerful few subdued the unpowerful many by threatening violence."

However, no all-encompassing novel would be complete without some mention of book shopping, and Franzen provides a few paragraphs on that as well. As a former professor, the financially strapped Chip is forced to unload his academic tomes for pennies on the dollar to come up with enough money to take his latest bimbo out on the weekend. Chip is also guilty of removing the $1 price sticker from the flyleaf of a remaindered book in order to better reciprocate the expensive silk shirt his sister has given him for Christmas.

With the exception of the talking-turd scene—a bizarre (and not funny) passage where the medicated and stupefied father confronts his personal demons in the form of a yapping pile of feces—*The Corrections* is impressive in its ability to capture the spirit of our times. Of course, what everyone really remembers about *The Corrections* is that Oprah Winfrey withdrew her invitation to interview Franzen when he failed to express sufficient gratitude after she had selected the novel for Oprah's Book Club.*

There was some criticism of Franzen for being too highbrow and elitist, but the bottom line for me is that *The Corrections* was a great book that wouldn't be widely read anyway, because somewhat bleak, 567-page novels about modern ennui never are. As a wag, I thought Oprah's rebuke of Franzen served as a sort of backhanded endorsement for discriminating readers like me—a marketing ploy that I wouldn't mind using for my own writings.

Coincidentally, the other big social book shopping novel of our times, Richard Ford's *Independence Day*

---

* *The Corrections* is still an Oprah Book Club designee.

Touring Franzen

I've read two other Franzen books, and they are also fine but in total contrast to *The Corrections*. *The Twenty-Seventh City* (1988) is a pot-boiler crime novel set in St. Louis, with political intrigue fueled by the conflicts of the different social classes in the city. (Franzen grew up near there.) It doesn't have the style, wit, and strength of voice of *The Corrections*, but it's well written and has a driving plot that carries the book. Franzen's compilation of essays titled *How to Be Alone* (2002) came out after *The Corrections*, and it includes "Why Bother?" and "Meet Me in St. Louis." The latter is his rebuttal essay to all the brouhaha surrounding being selected as an Oprah author. (I haven't finished his latest collection of essays, *The Discomfort Zone: A Personal History* [2006]. I thought the opening essay, "House for Sale," was good, but the ones after that started to remind me too much of Garrison Keillor.)

Book shopping-wise, I had a frustrating experience trying to obtain a copy of *How to Be Alone*. While in New York City, I was herded to the drinking holes of famous writers on a literary pub tour of Greenwich Village that included the White Horse Tavern, where Dylan Thomas drank himself to death. While staggering from one bar to another (a constantly full bladder; not drunk), I noticed a hardcover copy of *How to Be Alone* on a sidewalk table for six dollars. I waved at the tour leader to stop so I could buy the book, but the group marched on, determined to stay on schedule. Fearing being left behind in the city, I abandoned the purchase opportunity to rejoin the entourage. Didn't seem much like a lit tour after that.

(1995), had publicity problems as well. It began with the double-whammy surrounding Richard Ford. Not only does he have too common a name, but the title of his best book, *Independence Day*, can easily be confused with the summer blockbuster movie of the same name, which was released in 1996. Ford's novel is the story of the divorced writer-turned-real estate agent Frank Bascombe, who takes his estranged son to both the basketball and baseball Halls of Fame over the 4th of July weekend. It's a rich but slow-paced book that explores personal reconciliation, the importance of community, and the acceptance of difficult family situations. This is in contrast to the movie *Independence Day*, which depicts the human race barely surviving a shootout with some creatures from outer space. All that's left at the end of the film is a radioactive, charred rubble of a planet ruled by the triumvirate of Will Smith, Bill Pullman, and Judd Hirsch.

Ford is one of those authors (Anne Tyler is another) who make writing look easy, which is, of course, difficult to pull off. He has a conversational, nonchalant tone that draws me in. As I reread parts of the book, I can just flow with him for pages. Some people don't like his "non-style" style, but for me it's highly personal. I feel as if the character is talking to me—and in *Independence Day*, the main character and narrator, Frank Bascombe, tells us how he feels about everything and everyone, admitting to his own personal shortcomings, but not in a whiney, remorseful way.

I'm not alone in my admiration. One critic called *Independence Day*—and I love this phrase—a fin-de-siècle work, indicating that it captures American life in the late twentieth century. (It did win the Pulitzer Prize for fiction.) It makes sense. Instead of making his main character a writer or professor or someone rich and glamorous, Ford shows us how an ordinary guy tackles daily the painful issues of divorce, the numbness of the suburban American experience, and the trials of making a living.

With wit and wisdom, *Independence Day* asks the question, "How do we survive and rationalize our existence in the spiritual vacuum of modern life?" I've given this book as a gift to several people—once to a guy who I knew was going through a divorce. *Independence Day* has it all: insights on modern life, sports, and of course, book shopping.

The book shopping perspective, however, is different. It's not the view of a bargain hunter, but rather that of an author who stumbles upon his own work. Bascombe is staying overnight with his son in Coo-

Other Ford Works

Frank Bascombe also is the main character of an earlier Richard Ford novel, *The Sportswriter* (1986). I've read the novel, but I remember very little about it and even went so far as to use it for a book credit, a regrettable, hasty act, which I rectified by purchasing a replacement copy. In an attempt to recapture some of the same feelings I had for *Independence Day*, I reread part of *The Sportswriter*, but my bookmark tells me I quit after three chapters.

If you like *Independence Day*, *The Lay of the Land* (2006) is written in the same style and pace. (The time frame of the nearly 500-page book covers a Thanksgiving holiday weekend.) Frank Bascombe is older now (fifty-five), still a real-estate agent in New Jersey, and he has reached what he calls the Permanent Period, the time when you realize "so much of your life is in the books already." And yes, there is a cameo book shopping experience, when Bascombe, recovering from prostate cancer, is forced to urinate after-hours in the "darkened Colonial entryway of the Antiquarian Book Nook" while he gazes at "out-of-print, never-read Daphne du Mauriers and John O'Haras in vellum."

perstown, New York, at a local inn called the Deerslayer. Its musty old parlor is filled with stacks of *American Heritage* and *National Geographic* magazines, dated MLS booklets, and the complete works of James Fenimore Cooper. It is there that Bascombe, who was a writer twenty years earlier, runs across a copy of his own book of short stories. Ford writes:

> Nor is this the first time I've happened onto my book *blind*: church book sales, sidewalk tables in Gotham, yard sales in unlikely midwestern cities, one rain-soaked night on top of a trash can behind the Haddam Public Library, where I was groping around in the dark to find the after-hours drop-off. And once, to my dismay, in a friend's house shortly after he'd blown his brains out, though I never thought my book played a part. Once published, a book never strays so far from its author.

Eventually, the book reminds him of his previous life, not as a writer, but of the losses suffered earlier in his life (the death of a son and a subsequent divorce). Overcome by a rush of despair, he tosses the book across the room.

Although I've yet to run across a used copy of the only other book I've written (co-authored with Michael W. Berry), *Understanding Search Engines: Mathematical Modeling and Text Retrieval* (1999), I have witnessed a similar book shopping experience. I was with a friend's wife, the writer Laurie Blauner (see Chapter 6, "Master Control: The Influences of a Book Shopper Friend"), in a Seattle bookstore when we stumbled across her book of poems, *Self-Portrait With an Unwilling Landscape* (1989). Laurie seemed saddened by the sight of her book lost in the stacks. While I don't usually buy poetry—as a matter of fact, I never buy poetry—it seemed that rescuing the book for a few dollars was the decent thing

Jonathan Lethem: New and Used

Jonathan Lethem is one of those writers who, once he gets on your radar, he's all over your radar. I remember hearing about *Motherless Brooklyn* (1999), a detective noir fiction book, in which a small-time private detective/hood with Tourette's syndrome tries to solve the murder of his paternal boss. But this first mention of Lethem didn't register in my mind. It wasn't until I read Nick Hornby's *The Polysyllabic Spree* (2004), a compilation of his *Believer* magazine columns about reading, that I started putting the pieces together.

One of Hornby's columns praised Lethem's *The Fortress of Solitude* (2003), especially because it dealt with the racially charged story of a white kid who grows up in a predominantly black section of Brooklyn in the 1970s. I was pulled in by Lethem's grimy, lyrical prose, written in an oblique style that is challenging, but not overwhelming.

After *Fortress*, I soon read *Motherless Brooklyn*, which takes you within the battling mind of a person with Tourette's, but the book works as a detective novel as well. Coincidentally, in this same time frame I inadvertently discovered a Lethem essay about being a clerk in a used bookstore, in Marc Joseph's pictorial book *New and Used* (2006). In the essay, Lethem maintains that it was brash clerks like him who ruled these stores, not the clients or the owners. *New and Used* is a gorgeously printed book filled with pictures of used bookstore spaces and vinyl record stores. It captures that feeling you so crave in these places and qualifies as the best pictorial paean to reading this side of the book of André Kertész photographs entitled *On Reading* (originally published in 1971, and restored and reprinted in 2008).

I am still wondering why it took me so long to find Lethem, but it's comforting to know that even late in my reading life I can discover someone new (even though Lethem's been on the writing scene for years) and go gaga over him.

to do.* She seemed pleased, and she autographed it just as if it had been her latest novel. I don't think it is the financial aspect of losing royalties that causes an author to be taken aback when stumbling across a used copy of his or her own book. Seeing your book at a Friends of the Library rummage sale or in the unsecured rack in front of the neighborhood used bookstore must trigger a strong flashback to the memory of what was going on in your life at the time you were writing it. Of course, we readers experience those recurrences with our favorite books as well (ergo *The Book Shopper*), but writers must really get emotionally attached. In this way all books are social novels, reflecting the lives of those writing and reading them.

* Rescuing one book from obscurity is a "noble" gesture, as long as you don't think about all the other worthy books being left behind, like the passed over pets at an animal shelter.

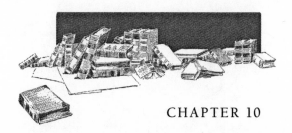

CHAPTER 10

Humorists: Being Funny Can Be Such a Chore

WHEN IT COMES TO modern literature, I have many gaps and holes in my knowledge, but when it comes to humor, my understanding runs thick and deep—and wide, too. Don't forget wide.* While some kids read comic books, I grew up reading *Mad* magazine. It was the only printed kid material available at my maternal grandmother's house, and my cousin and I would sit for hours in Grandma's worn recliner (she was probably sacrificing her favorite chair), reading and rereading the few tattered *Mad* anthologies that she kept within easy reach. This was in contrast to my paternal grandmother's house, where such mindless offerings were nonexistent, and humor was confined to my grandfather's long narratives about local rascals like himself, delivered as he lay on his favorite recliner (it had a vibrator feature). My cousin

---

* If you're looking for Garrison Keillor in this chapter, by the way, don't bother. I know it's heresy not to adore Keillor (similar to not liking Tom Hanks), but his brand of homespun humor has grown tiresome to this Midwesterner.

could recite lengthy passages from issues of *Mad* the way kids used to be able to recite poems or biblical verse. Armed with a *Mad*-derived sense of satire and spoof, we were able to survive middle school and high school; surviving, however, is not the same as flourishing.

But even with such credentials, I think analyzing humor is a doomed endeavor. It's much too subjective and dependent on the changing times. Every book shopper knows that this year's laughter is destined to populate, within a twelve to eighteen month time frame, the shelves of used bookstores everywhere (think *Fatherhood* [1986] by Bill Cosby or Paul Reiser's *Couplehood* [1994]). Perhaps the most recent example of a comic icon turned stale is *The Daily Show's America (The Book): A Citizen's Guide to Democracy Inaction* (2004), which will soon replace *Doonesbury* anthologies in the oversized, outdated Humor/Comedy bins. On the eve of the 2004 election between George W. Bush and John Kerry, *The Daily Show* with host Jon Stewart, along with Steven Colbert, Samantha Bee, and others, was a nightly entertainment phenomenon, tapping into this country's frustration with the government that dragged us into "Mess-o-potamia." As expected, a companion book, in the form of a satirical civics textbook, was published and made the bestseller list. Stewart hit the promotional circuit, including an appearance on C-SPAN, which marked the first time I ever videotaped a program on that station. Though a fan of *The Daily Show* when I can see it (I balk at paying big dollars for premium cable), I think the humor in the book was sophomoric.* Still, I'll probably hold on to my copy, which I received as a gift, for a while. I doubt it will emerge as one of the all-time greats like the original *National Lampoon 1964 High School Yearbook Parody* (1974), but some clever people worked on *America*, and who knows how their careers will be viewed twenty years hence. If Ronald Reagan, Arnold Schwarzenegger, and Jesse Ventura can hold high public office, would Steven Colbert as vice president in 2016 be so unimaginable?

I'm probably being unfair to *America*, because I hold all satires to the lofty standards set by *Yearbook*. Over the years, I've remained fascinated by this particular parody, even though I wasn't a rabid fan of the magazine. Written by P. J. O'Rourke, who went on to write some witty books (*Parliament of Whores: A Lone Humorist Attempts to Explain the Entire U.S. Government* [1991] and *Age and Guile Beat Youth, Innocence, and a Bad Haircut* [1996]), and Doug Kenney, who went on to cowrite such movies as *Animal House* and *Caddyshack*, it only takes a peek inside to rekindle my interest. Also on the staff of the *National Lampoon* parody were Michael O'Donoghue (Mr. Mike of *Saturday Night Live* fame), Christopher Cerf (son of Bennett), and the less well-known David Kaestle. Kaestle was the art director who, along with Michael Gross, was responsible for

---

* For example, the book has a classroom activity of dressing naked Supreme Court justice paper dolls in their robes.

the "look and feel" of the book as a cover-to-cover time capsule of the Midwest, circa 1964.

The setting is Estes Kefauver High School in Dacron, Ohio, the Mobile Home Capital of America. The artists even recreated ads in the back of the yearbook for Mr. Drippy ice cream and the Donna Gay Apparel clothing shop. What holds the book together is its narrative quality. The graduating seniors, among them the psycho, the foreign student, the class clown, the class slut, the rich kid, and the nice guy foil, appear throughout the book in pictures and in little blurbs that look like handwritten personal inscriptions. These characters give the book some depth. There are recurring faculty members as well, including history teacher Curtis Dittwiley and health teacher Duane Postum "played" by O'Rourke and Kenney respectively. Topping off the production is (intentional) bad photography and (intentional) lame writing, just like the awful pictures and prose endemic to every high-school yearbook ever produced. Intentional bad writing is difficult to pull off. It's like when an actor pretends to be a bad actor (Mark Wahlberg as porn star Dirk Diggler in *Boogie Nights* comes to mind). Because the book works on many levels, it has retained its cult status, and first editions are still bought and sold as rare books. (The book was reprinted several years ago as a 39th Reunion issue, but the repackaging and printing is horrible.)

Beyond the humor, I am still intrigued by the synergistic nature of the writing on display. Writing is not normally a group activity, and different writers may have different takes on the same subject. This can make collaborative work seem uneven. *Yearbook*, however, was one of those powerful combinations of writers and artists—like the Beatles—who came together for a relatively short period of time to create something beyond the sum of their parts.*

One of the better books in the "behind the laughs" genre is *Monty Python Speaks!* (1999), by David Morgan. It's not as easy to find as *The Complete Monty Python's Flying Circus: All the Words, Vols. 1 & 2* (1989), the scripts of every Monty Python routine, which are a handy reference for aficionados who must get the lines absolutely correct. *Speaks* is the book to read if you're interested in how the troupe engaged with each other while writing and acting in the four-season, forty-four-episode *Flying Circus* series and how *The Holy Grail* and *Life of Brian* came about. Morgan doesn't upstage his interviewees or make sweeping pronouncements about their genius and wit. He simply asks the right questions and lets the Pythons (all except Graham Chapman, who had died ten years earlier) reminisce. You get a sense of how the sketches were written and how the members worked (Michael Palin paired with Terry Jones, John Cleese with Chapman, while Eric Idle and ani-

---

* I am still shopping for a suitable copy of *Going Too Far* (1987), by Tony Hendra, or the more recent *A Futile and Stupid Gesture: How Doug Kenney and National Lampoon Changed Comedy Forever* (2006), by Josh Karp, both of which supposedly give accounts of those *Lampoon* days.

A Few Favorite Yuks

Here are a few of my all-time favorites. Some of those listed below aren't pure prose since often I like graphic elements mixed in:

- *MacDoodle St.* (1980), by Mark Alan Stamaty. A bustling streets of New York serial about Malcolm Frazzle, a dishwasher and a poet for *Dishwasher's Monthly.* Stamaty went on to do a cartoon about books for the *New York Times Book Review* for a short period of time.
- *How to Make Yourself Miserable* (1966), by Dan Greenburg and Marcia Jacobs. A combination cartoon and self-help book about how we go out of our way to be our own worst enemy.
- *The Best of Modern Humor* (1983), edited by Mordecai Richler. You can find it in most used bookstores for about a buck. It has an excerpt from Dan Greenburg's classic *How to Be a Jewish Mother,* an ode to Jewish mothers' ability to "plant, cultivate and harvest guilt." The collection also includes Nora Ephron's "A Few Words About Breasts." Originally published in *Esquire* in 1973, the essay solidified Ephron's career as a humorist slash essayist. *Humor* also

mator Terry Gilliam each worked alone). There are also interviews with those who orbited Planet Python: Ian MacNaughton, their director and producer, Carol Cleveland, who was often cast when a real voluptuous female was needed instead of a Python contains notable works by Ian Frazier ("Dating Your Mom") and Bruce Jay Friedman (see below).

- *Holidays on Ice* (1997), by David Sedaris. I was a slow convert to Sedaris because I never listened to NPR much after my stint at a public radio station. However, the original *Holidays on Ice*, with a cover photo of Santa at a urinal, caught my attention. It contains Sedaris's breakthrough essay about being a Christmas elf at Macy's and the piece in which a newspaper critic pans local Christmas theater productions. (Sedaris's publishers added more material and reissued the book in 2008 under the same name.)

- *The Collected Short Fiction of Bruce Jay Friedman* (1995). Another book worth grabbing for a dollar or two, so you only have to ask yourself, "Is it worth the shelf space?" I'm glad I kept my reviewer's copy, so I could reread the story about the guy who takes in a worn-out Sammy Davis Jr. so the entertainer can get some well-deserved rest. Another memorable piece is the one where a therapy patient tests his doctor's commitment to confidentiality by murdering the therapist's wife. A lot of the stories are kind of throwback New York-type stuff. John Cheever meets Woody Allen.

(continued on next page)

in drag, and David Sherlock, Chapman's longtime companion. All add their observations to round out and verify what the Pythons say about each other.

Speaks focuses on the writing process itself, the importance of cadence, of choosing the right word,

- *The Evolution Man, Or, How I Ate My Father* (1993) is unusual because author Roy Lewis is able to sustain a single narrative line of pure humor. Originally published in England in 1960, Pantheon re-released the book in 1993 only to see it buried on remainder tables by 1996. Much of Lewis's humor comes from his mastery of understatement. *Evolution Man* remains unbelievably current, which can be attributed to its prehistorical subject matter—a witty account of cave life by an articulate ape boy named Ernest. Along with his primitive free-thinking father, Ernest is dedicated to moving the human species from the Pleistocene epoch to the late Pleistocene epoch. The book debates such age-old questions as whether it's better to have a large brain or retractable claws, live in a tree or a cave, and the advantages and disadvantages of mating with someone not from your immediate horde.

and of compromising to please the group as a whole, not just the more dominant individuals. It was an environment seemingly free of rivalries like those of The Not Ready for Prime Time players chronicled in *Saturday Night: A Backstage History of Saturday Night Live* (1986), by Doug Hill and Jeff Weingrad. This is not to say that the Pythons weren't temperamental or didn't disagree with each other (Cleese v. Jones was quite common), but they genuinely seemed to like each other. *Speaks* captures a sense of creative camaraderie that reassures the Python viewer with the comfy knowledge that our comic heroes weren't a bunch of insecure assholes.

Being part of such a creative group sounds like an idyllic experience, but I'm not sure a participant fully appreciates the moment until it is past. I wonder if the folks working on *Saturday Night Live*, *National Lampoon*, *Monty Python*, or even *The Daily Show* circa 2004 were fully aware that for a relatively brief moment they were at the zenith of their powers. Did they understand the rarity of this great convergence of comic talents at their peak combined with a public that craved their brand of humor?

Despite humorists' complaints that society dismisses them (similar to the I-get-no-respect shtick that athletes use to motivate themselves against their next opponent),* they have always deserved—since the day I sat in my grandma's recliner and read magazines with my cousin—the same accolades, barbs, and expectations I bestow on others. It is with this in mind that I pursue their works with the same book shopping zeal I give to "grownup" writers.

---

* One of the most well-known lines is Woody Allen's: "When you do comedy, you're not sitting at the grownups' table."

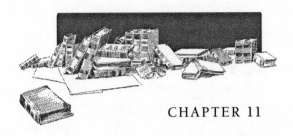

CHAPTER 11

Larry McMurtry: Patron Saint of Book Shoppers

LARRY MCMURTRY POSES SOME major problems for the book shopper. His prose is boundless, his style accessible, his books multitudinous. He cranks out Wild West westerns, modern day westerns, tales of youth, updates on tales of youth, all of which predictably pass through the cycle of being published en masse, remaindered, then showing up in used bookstores in heavy numbers. One could probably do a separate *Book Shopper* on McMurtry alone, or at least combine him with another high production writer such as Joyce Carol Oates, literature's answer outputwise to Barbara Cartland. With the exception of *All My Friends Are Going to Be Strangers* (1972), the story of a young writer sweating it out at Rice University in the 1950s, most of McMurtry's earlier, thinner works like *The Last Picture Show* (1966), *Leaving Cheyenne* (1963), and *Horseman, Pass By* (1961) have been squeezed off the shelves of used bookstores by his later, more voluminous works.

McMurtry's western writing, highlighted by his best and most popular book, *Lonesome Dove* (1985), is much easier to find. I am still in awe of how readable *Dove* is—it may be the easiest to read 900-page book ever written. As a firm believer that seeing a screen version of a book stunts the reader's imagination, I always felt fortunate that I read *Dove* before I saw the made-for-TV movie.* I did like the miniseries, starring Tommy Lee Jones as Woodrow Call and Robert Duvall as Augustus McCrae, two former Texas Rangers who drive a herd of longhorns from the Rio Grande to Montana. I loved the part where Woodrow beats the hell out of the bullies who pick on his son, and Gus's deathbed scene is a tearjerker that rivals Debra Winger's signoff in the film adaptation of another McMurtry book, *Terms of Endearment* (1975). (Have I revealed too much for you? C'mon, you've had at least twenty years to read those McMurtry works or see them on the tube.) Still, I wish there would be a restriction that allowed only McMurtry's mediocre books like *Anything for Billy* (1988), a western that chronicles the

* My favorite book-to-film adaptation is George Roy Hill's 1972 production of Kurt Vonnegut's *Slaughterhouse-Five* (1965), which featured supporting performances by Ron Leibman (Rachel's father on *Friends*) and the pulchritudinous Valerie Perrine, and a musical score by pianist Glenn Gould. Hill also directed *Butch Cassidy and the Sundance Kid*, *The Sting*, and *Slap Shot*.

life of Billy the Kid through the eyes of a writer of dime westerns, to be used as fodder for the cinema. A well-written book creates an evocative setting in the reader's mind, which the film version always compromises.

In addition to his books' sheer availability, another reason that McMurtry is held in such high esteem by used book shoppers is that he once owned an antique bookstore in Washington, D.C., and now runs an even more intriguing business called Booked Up Inc.* This venture houses thousands of used and rare books in several old warehouse-sized buildings in McMurtry's hometown of Archer City, Texas. (There's a photo of Booked Up in Marc Joseph's *New and Used*.) Naturally, I'd like to make a pilgrimage to Archer City to see the largest collection of used books this side of the Goodwill National Library, and if I'm ever in Oklahoma City and looking for a day trip . . .

However, according to their website, Booked Up doesn't stock all that voluminous McMurtry fiction, which is okay by me, because I've reached the point where I refuse to read any more of it. This happened after I had to review the 750-page *Comanche Moon* (1997), the sequel to *Streets of Laredo* (1993), which

---

* A Dallas newspaper reporter wrote a feature story about running into McMurtry at Booked Up. She generously describes his demeanor as "not particularly friendly" and his answers to her questions as "succinct." Another example of "Book Lovers Are Not Necessarily People Lovers."

was itself the sequel to *Lonesome Dove*. *Comanche Moon* featured the early ranger days of Gus and Woodrow as they rode aimlessly over the barren plains chasing some bloodthirsty (but spiritually centered) Comanches. In summary, McMurtry took the big Texas longhorn literary legacy that he established with *Lonesome Dove* and cooked it down to a carcass.

My moratorium on McMurtry fiction also holds for his other later books like *Texasville* (1987), the sequel to *The Last Picture Show*; *Duane's Depressed* (1999), the sequel to *Texasville*; *Some Can Whistle* (1989), the sequel to *All My Friends Are Going to Be Strangers*; and *The Evening Star* (1992), the sequel to *Terms of Endearment*. McMurtry can't seem to let a good story end.

Nonfiction McMurtry

I much prefer McMurtry's nonfiction. Several of his nonfiction works are quite good, especially a book of essays about Hollywood written for *American Film* magazine and titled *Film Flam: Essays on Hollywood* (1987). I picked up a copy for three bucks and buzzed through it in a few days. McMurtry, who was the screenwriter for the film versions of *The Last Picture Show* and *Terms of Endearment*, gives us a clear, and sometimes humorous, look at the Hollywood mentality—at least, what it was like twenty-five years ago. The following clip is taken from *Film*

Flam, where McMurtry describes life in the screening room.

> Seeing a movie at a screening is far from an ideal method. Generally, there will be a tense producer at one elbow, a hypertense director at the other, and six or seven grim PR people scattered around, all of them expecting one to come forth with both incisive analysis and wild praise, some eight or ten seconds after "The End" has appeared on the screen. One can stall a moment by yawning, or stretching, but ultimately comment will have to be made. I quickly settled on a tactic which I had previously used only when viewing best friends' babies, which is to look jolly and say, "Well, that's *some* baby," with a touch of emphasis on the *some*. "Well, that's *some* film," is the perfect deflecting remark, because the producer and the director will not much care what the writer thinks anyway; once assured that he is not going to spit on them in disgust, they usually forget the writer and go right back to talking about advertising, openings, etc.

Although the book is primarily about screenwriting, it is also about novel writing, as he compares the two throughout the book.

My interest in McMurtry's screenwriting was rekindled recently when he won the Oscar, along with his frequent collaborator, Diana Ossana, for the screen adaptation of Annie Proulx's story "Brokeback Mountain." I went to see *Brokeback Mountain* to sample again McMurtry's work as a screenwriter. The Ang Lee film is a worthy representation of the Proulx story and captures a sense of life in the West and the ill-fated longing of two men (and their wives) for love.* A companion book, *Brokeback Mountain: Story to Screenplay*, was published in 2005. This slim volume contains the Proulx short story, the screenplay, and essays by Proulx, McMurtry, and Ossana that reveal how the book was translated to the screen. (It's also a literary love fest between three writers who respect and admire each other very, very much.) An interesting passage is McMurtry's reference to his own *Film Flam*, where he opines that the best novels sometimes have a literary style that is difficult to capture on screen. (Our film expectations of great books may also be too high.) Novels also can be lengthy, which forces screenwriters to delete many scenes. According to McMurtry, short stories like "Brokeback Mountain," with its terse, desolate style, may prove less difficult to adapt for the screen.

A better place to find a copy of "Brokeback Mountain" is in a fine little collection that McMurtry edited called *Still Wild: Short Fiction of the American West—1950 to the Present* (2000). *Still Wild* also includes Richard Ford's "Rock Springs" and Robert Boswell's "Glissando." The latter is a heartbreaking story of a fourteen-year-old boy's reconciliation of the sadness and goodness that is his father, while the two travel together. Boswell is not covered in *The*

---

* But while watching *Brokeback Mountain,* I was dying for a chuckle, some relief from the depression. The movie needed a laugh track or something to break the never-ending sadness. I haven't seen a movie so in need of a yuk since Lee's *Ice Storm.*

Book Shopper because I'm still hunting for a copy of his out-of-print collection, *Living to Be a Hundred* (1994), where "Glissando" originally appeared.

Another fascinating book by McMurtry is *Walter Benjamin at the Dairy Queen: Reflections at Sixty and Beyond* (1999), a series of essay-like chapters on the author's self-discovery as a writer. McMurtry examines the combination of memory, childhood events, and education that made him such a prodigious writer. The chapter describing his reactions to heart-bypass surgery deserves special recognition because it showcases McMurtry's clear, clean style. He avoids medical jargon and sentimentality while relating how this drastic, highly invasive surgery temporarily obliterated his sense of self and soul.

Walter Benjamin also shows us the early influences on McMurtry. From his father, a rancher in Archer City, the young McMurtry heard tales of local cowboys that would later be the foundations of his western characters. He also attributes his love of writing to a box of nineteen books he received from his cousin, who dropped them off on his way to the Army. McMurtry mentions other early favorites such as the ten-volume *My Book House* and a set of the World Book Encyclopedia that his parents purchased for their home. (The former was my first exposure to the classics, too, a gift, as I have said, from my grandmother to our family.)

If these aren't enough reasons to pick up a copy of *Benjamin*, there are book shopper anecdotes as well. McMurtry writes about books and bookshops as if

Used Book Butchery

Many fates befall books other than being read and treasured. —Richard Ford, *Independence Day*

All used books should avoid Greeneville, Tennessee. Located in the northeastern corner of the state, Greeneville is the home of our 17th President, Andrew Johnson (he succeeded the fallen Lincoln), and it has a decent downtown with some quaint Greek-revival architecture. It also has a ho-hum replica of the cabin where Johnson was born, and the General Morgan Inn and Conference Center, where my friend Denise and I stopped for lunch on our way to Jonesborough, Tennessee. Named after the dashing Confederate cavalry general John Hunt Morgan, who was shot and killed near Greeneville, the inn impressed me at first sight with its wonderfully restored Southern elegance. The dining room had tall ceilings and white tablecloths, but its "library" décor turned out to be faux. Instead of shelves lined with books, the owners just tacked up thin boards, like ornamental baseboards, to look like shelves. Moreover, they had torn the cloth spines off of books and glued them on the fake shelves to make a grand fake library. There were book spines of the works of Leo Tolstoy and Graham Greene, along with *Reader's Digest* condensed books and several sets of encyclopedias. As Denise said later, it was disturbing—like trying to eat in a room decorated with kitten skins.

they were women: "My fascination was with books, the way they looked, hefted, were printed, smelled, and of course, what was inside them." *Benjamin* is written for those who appreciate books and reading, but don't like gushiness.*

I particularly appreciate McMurtry's admission that he has written his share of bargain bin books: "I think two or three of my books are good, just as he [McMurtry's father] thought two or three of the many horses that he owned were good. The rest of my writing may well end up in that great City of Dead Words on the old fiction floor of Acres of Books in Cincinnati." This is the only time I've run across an established writer's acknowledgment of the inconsistency in his or her own work. An important theme running through *The Book Shopper* is that writers are often inconsistent in their output, and it may be unrealistic to expect more.

His admission of his inconsistency, along with his attempt to build a used bookstore Mecca on the Oklahoma-Texas border, makes McMurtry my patron saint of book shoppers. And it's all right for our deities to be flawed. A few lousy books, perhaps

---

* Naturally, it wouldn't be Larry McMurtry if he didn't try to do a sequel or a prequel to a successful work. After the critically acclaimed *Benjamin,* similar nonfiction books appeared and reappeared: *Roads: Driving America's Great Highways* (2000) and *In a Narrow Grave,* which was a collection of personal essays originally published in 1968 and then reprinted and updated in 2001.

less than a great business sense (Booked Up has suffered some economic setbacks), even a little crabby at times—these shortcomings only make them more human and endearing.

PART THREE

What Next?
Read, Store, or Sell?

CHAPTER 12

Books as Gifts

*And I am sure I am not alone when I state that cavalierly
foisting unsolicited reading material upon book lovers is
like buying underwear for people you hardly know.*
—Joe Queenan, "Wish List: No More Books!"

IF BOOK GIVING IS presumptuous, as book critic
Joe Queenan implies, might there be some dispen-
sation given to those who forgo giving new books
and instead redistribute used or remaindered (which
look like new) copies? This is a dilemma I have pon-
dered since the day I was in a campus bookstore and
overheard a guy boasting to his female companion,
"I am really good at picking out hidden gems for my
friends." He stumbled across a travel book and said
something like "Eureka! Here's a good one, I bet so-
and-so would like it! Hmmm. Five dollars." Then the
guy set the book down and didn't buy it.

I considered the possible rationales behind that
action. Did he have a problem with appearing to be
cheap? If this was the case, couldn't he have removed
the price tag and stuck a bow over the gummy res-

idue? Maybe his friend wasn't worth five bucks—a sad commentary on the value of that friendship. On the other hand, perhaps he was himself a saturated Joe Queenan-like collector and realized that a consumable gift, such as a bag of nuts, or a practical one, such as windshield-washer fluid, would be more appreciated.

Despite the fact that I enjoy pondering these possibilities, none of this deters me from giving away books. I'm just not so cavalier about it. I believe that (in the words of Maxine Hong Kingston) "it takes skill to give gifts."

Although I did remove the shameful "40% Off" supermarket tag for *Rhett Butler's People* (2007) when I picked it up as a Christmas gift for my mother, who had been waiting over half a century for a decent sequel to *Gone with the Wind*, I usually leave the price tags on books.* My rationale for leaving any price reduction notations in place is quite simple. Just as I'm wary of getting books that I didn't specifically ask for, I'm equally aware that close friends may feel a sense of obligation to read something I purchase for them. So as I hand over a gift book I say, "Look I only paid two ninety-nine for this, so if you don't like it, pitch it." This takes away most of the pressure on the recipient to read the book, and

---

* The problem was that the tag identified the book as having come from a supermarket. Fortunately, my mother is oblivious to my whole book shopper thing.

he or she can accept the gift as a suggestion, not a directive.

Of course, it's never quite as simple as it sounds, and I have wrestled with several variations of the book-giving dilemma. Recently, I needed a Christmas gift for one of the family boyfriends, who had just graduated mid-year with a bachelor's degree in computer science. My first thought was to go for the consumables, in his case maybe a frozen pizza, but then I figured since this kid had a busy mind, he might enjoy *Gödel, Escher, Bach*, the much acclaimed tome by Douglas Hofstadter that compares the works of the mathematician Kurt Gödel, the artist M. C. Escher, and the composer Johann Sebastian Bach. Heralded as a classic back when it was first published in 1979, *GEB* is still in print. I owned a used copy that I had picked up for under five bucks in an impulsive moment when I thought I needed something to dramatically improve my mind. It would have been easy for me to part with such a book under the circumstances, but I wondered if I was being a little cheap—even for one of the transient family boyfriends—and I didn't want to burden him with an unsolicited book. I decided to give him a new copy of the book, but I left the gift receipt inside for an easy exchange. While he opened his gift, I studied his reaction for feigned pleasure. If I thought he was just being polite (commendable to think that he liked me enough to mislead me), I'd strongly suggest that he just return it and find something else. If his reaction was a bit warmer, I'd sug-

gest, "Hey! I've got an extra used copy at home you
can have, and thank you for freeing up some valuable shelf space. Take the new copy and exchange it
for a couple of Lindt chocolates or a DVD of anime."
Either I was completely fooled or he was fascinated
by the book. In any case, I'm still stuck with my
used and unread copy of *GEB*.

Another instance of the book-giving conun-
drum came up during this same Christmas with my
younger daughter, Bonnie. I noticed on her Amazon
wish list that in addition to wanting Dansko shoes,
she wanted some books, including Tracy Kidder's
*Mountains Beyond Mountains: The Quest of Dr. Paul
Farmer, a Man Who Would Cure the World* (2003).
Coincidentally, I already had a hardcover copy in
pristine condition that was primed to be unloaded,
since it read like one of those books that seem better suited as a long feature article in a magazine. (My
older daughter abandoned it to my study for the same
reason.) So I wrapped it up and planned to explain
the book's origins to Bonnie as she opened her gift.
I didn't even get the words of explanation out of my
mouth, though. After her initial delight, she looked
me right in the eye with the steely intimidating
glance only daughters can manage, and demanded
to know, "Did you book shop this?" "Yes," I admitted warily. She smiled again and said, "Good!" with
no further explanation. Looking back now, I think
of this as a Bonnie-as-chip-off-the-ol'-Book-Shopper-
block moment. That is, I interpreted her reaction
as an indication that she understood *me*, or more

accurately, a part of me.* I recognize my satisfaction with this little scenario to be a reversal of the universal desire we have as children for our parents to understand us. It was a connection forged not by a book but by the behind-the-scenes act that went into selecting that book.

If you can set aside the dual barriers of worrying whether one (a) appears cheap or (b) is oppressing another with unwanted recommendations, a personal library can become a kind of book warehouse, with same-day shipping. It's an excuse to become even more of a book shopper, with license to pick up several copies of perennial favorites in case, for example, my older daughter, Cynthia, needs an extra copy of Mary Karr's *Liars' Club* or Ian Frazier's *Great Plains* for a friend as a token of appreciation. I try to keep my shelves well stocked in case the need arises.

All this used book gift giving assumes, of course, that any used book that you give doesn't have a heartfelt inscription tattooed on the inside cover or title page that reveals the fluid nature of relationships. If you read a handwritten inscription that says, "This is my favorite book, dear friend, I hope you like it," or "To my darling son, Happy Birthday, you mean so much to me," you know that things have changed in that relationship for better or (probably) worse.

---

* It seems unfair to expect people to understand everything about us, when we don't even understand ourselves completely.

It is for these reasons that I rarely inscribe a book when I give it as a gift: I don't like to restrict its potential for commerce. It seems hypocritical of me to give a friend a book and hurt his or her ability to unload it with the greatest possible ease. Conversely, when someone gives me such an inscribed book, I keep it well beyond its usefulness. A good example is my copy of Dick Butkus's autobiography, *Butkus: Flesh and Blood* (1997). I do not keep this book because I need to constantly refer to descriptions of how the Hall of Fame Chicago Bear linebacker turned some ball carrier's shoulder into oatmeal or how he made a quarterback's head recoil. Rather, I keep it because it holds my brother's note on how he waited in line to get the sneering Butkus's autograph. Another one of my favorite personal inscriptions is book shopper Dave's mini review of *Last Exit to Brooklyn* (1964), which included a rewrite in his own hand of several blurbs from reviewers, topped off with his own assessment of *Last Exit*. "It ain't pretty, but it is one hell of a book." Even if I didn't think *Last Exit* was a tour de force of bleakness, I'd hang on to the book because it reminds me so much of Dave.*

At this stage you might be thinking, "Pity the fool who tries to buy Murray a book," and on the surface this is true. For the most part, rather than end-

---

* See Chapter 6, "Master Control: The Influences of a Book Shopper Friend."

ing up sounding as irascible as Joe Queenan, I try to discourage people from giving me surprise books as gifts. I do this either by providing them (if asked) with a specific book suggestion (title-author-condition), or I mention that I am much more in need of clothes, an area of expression where I am far less particular and have plenty of room for improvement.

Nevertheless, Queenan makes several good points in his diatribe against the giving of books, one of which is that all serious readers keep lists of books that we hope to read in our lifetime, and there is a finite number of books we can expect to read. (He calculates that number as 2,138.) He says that every time someone gives us a book we "really must read," that challenges our own list. Queenan does admit that not all gift books are bad, citing as examples the crime detective novels his sisters gave him.

For me, I do want to limit what gets foisted my way, but I don't want to eliminate those exquisite moments where the surprise literary gift has been a connecting moment to another person. There are certain books, ranging from *The Golden Book of the Civil War* (1960), from my parents, to Oscar Hijuelos's *Mr. Ives' Christmas* (1995), from my longtime companion Denise, to Siegfried Kracauer's *Theory of Film: The Redemption of Physical Reality* (1960),* a gift from my daughter Cynthia for my fifty-second birthday, that have stood out along the book-gifting

---

* Coincidentally, Kracauer is a contemporary of Walter Benjamin. See Chapter 11, "Larry McMurtry: Patron Saint of Book Shoppers."

Gifts Unaccepted

During the brief, frantic, dot.com craze, I worked for a boss of Cuban descent who was both a little high strung and a trumpet player (kind of like the Mambo Kings' Nestor and Cesar rolled into one). I remember driving to lunch with him as a blaring brass cacophony blasted through his car's speakers —bleating, non-melodic, and intense. ("The music in my head," he said.) He told me once that if he became wealthy (all dot.commers bought into this promise, including me) he'd quit and play the trumpet. He could be tough to work for at times, but I felt he had a good heart. In our two years together, he tried to mold me into a product development wiz, and I wanted to encourage him to appreciate some of the potential richness in his own life. One day when he was leaving for a vacation at the beach with his family, I gave him a copy of Hijuelos's *Mambo Kings* as a gift. When he returned to the office, he told me that he hadn't read a word.

As the days of the dot.com boom approached an end, he loaned me a copy of the Spencer Johnson bestseller *Who Moved My Cheese?* (1998), about career planning and understanding changes in one's life. I looked over the *Cheese* book, which tells the story of two cute-as-buttons mice (never referred to as "vermin") and two Little People, who all live and work happily in a maze (never referred to as "the rat race") until someone moves their cheese, the cheese being a metaphor for their livelihood or job. After the cheese is moved, the mice proactively hunt for new cheese, find it, and are happy again. The Little People, however, are reluctant to move forward; they insist on returning again and again to the same spot in the maze (now devoid of cheese) and whining ad nauseam. One of the Little People eventually gets with the program, but the other Little Person—well, we never find out what happens to him. (Just like we never discover exactly *who* moved the cheese.)

Even worse than the book's insipid prose is the ominous underlying message: Hey, the Man can jack your cheese all over the maze, and it's your responsibility to deal with it. In other words, "UPPER MANAGEMENT IS NOT ACCOUNTABLE FOR ANYTHING WE DO." To my mind, this explains why the book is so popular—it rationalizes any action management takes.

When *Cheese* books start circulating around the office, pink slips are not far off, and my case was no different, through no fault of my boss. A few years later the company was sold off and closed, but my former boss and I kept in touch and even began to meet for an occasional coffee and to chat about our futures and our families, leaving Hijuelos and *Cheese* behind.

trail. I only hope that a significant percentage of the books I have subjected others to over the years have brought some pleasure to their recipients.

My advice is this: If you must buy books for others, put some serious thought into both the recipient and the book, and then ignore the fear that I (and Joe Queenan) might have instilled in you. And if you need a little extra value-added reassurance that you're doing the right thing, be sure to include with your gift book an accompanying bookmark—preferably something that "can't miss"—like a supermarket gift card.

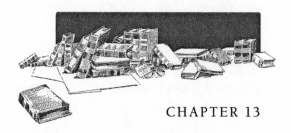

CHAPTER 13

The Classic Book Group

I've never been much of a book group joiner. As a matter of fact, I've never been much of a joiner of anything—churches, fraternities, professional organizations. With book groups or "reading clubs" (as I sometimes refer to them, because the dominating participants often beat the quieter members over the head with their views or book selections), I have the same reticence. Despite the enjoyment I derive from talking and hearing about books and reading, I have a natural contrariety that keeps me from belonging to much of anything. With book groups it's been a lifelong dilemma whether to avoid them altogether, join one, or organize my own.

It all began in the early eighties, when I was still married, and before my wife and I had children and thus felt it necessary to go to church.* We joined a Sunday morning Books, Wine, and Cheese Group, hosted by a wiry, thick-bearded hippie in the windowless, basement-bar of his duplex. A Vietnam vet,

* I think it is important to instill values in children, which they can later reject.

he seemed to be a happy-go-lucky type who once admitted that he missed Southeast Asia—or at least missed the prices he paid for booze and pot while in the service.

I was lured to the group by the promising first book in the series, William Faulkner's *Light in August*. Faulkner was an author I felt I should read, or should have read, but the prose had seemed impenetrable when I was an undergraduate, and I welcomed the opportunity for some assistance. Unfortunately, after Faulkner, the group soon degenerated into reading Robert Ludlum potboilers and the like. The only other book I remember enjoying was a well-written Ernest Hemingway knockoff titled *Matador*, written in 1952 by Barnaby Conrad. When my turn came to select, I chose Thomas Pynchon's *The Crying of Lot 49* (1966), a suggestion greeted by a chorus of ignorance, disgust, and disapproval.

I don't recall learning anything about the wine or cheese, except that I wasn't worth a damn the rest of the day. I wasn't even fit to read Robert Ludlum books, and as I found out later, neither was our host. After one of the meetings, the bottle of wine my wife and I had brought remained unopened, and we decided to just leave it as a gift to our host for tolerating this weekly invasion. But his young wife, who worked as a waitress and sometimes apologized for not understanding whatever book we were reading, gave us a pleading look as we were heading out the door and whispered, "Please take it. He doesn't need it." At that moment it became clear that the carefree host spent his Sunday afternoons cleaning up after the book group, bottle after bottle.

I don't think I stayed in the group long after that. I'd like to say in some wise, reflective way that I left because I didn't want to enable someone's destructive behavior, but I don't think I saw things like that back then. More likely, it was two other factors that swayed my leaving: my first daughter was soon to be born, and I did find reading books that were selected by consensus somewhat oppressive. Of course, the irony of this statement escaped me back then, since I was the person who subjected a small group of innocent readers to Thomas Pynchon.

The reason I share this confession is because it reminds me of the hold that Pynchon had for us literary-wannabes in the 1970s. First of all, he was the famous recluse who shunned the literary establishment, not only by being incommunicado but also by possessing a hip, erudite, word-playing and world-encompassing style. Who wouldn't want to be a famous writer who could riff on any subject in an all-knowing smart-ass tone? Of course, his style came at the expense of readability, and his novels lacked engaging characters or driving plots, but Pynchon had cachet, which I eagerly sought to mimic—and it wasn't just me. Since then, a review of any zany writer who takes you down rabbit holes of techno-babble, abstruseness, or paranoia inevitably mentions Pynchon or uses the adjective "Pynchonesque."

Unfortunately, trying to emulate this unorthodox manner probably set me back as a writer about fifteen years. I imitated his odd character names, such as Clayton "Bloody" Chiclitz, Mike Fallopian, and Oedipa Maas, in my own work (Dwight Kommatoss and Virginia Macaroon), and I still have trouble laying off tangential asides and parenthetical add-ons (don't cha know). But I don't blame Pynchon for stunting my growth. I still like him and use some of his lines in my vernacular; however, he's not someone you can recommend to others in good conscience. This has not prevented me from picking up copies of *Gravity's Rainbow* (1973), some for as little as a dime, in hopes of some day forming my own Thomas Pynchon reading group.

In anticipation of this improbable event, I have even purchased several Pynchon reading guides at full price. One of the better guides, actually, is a pocket paperback by Joseph Slade titled simply *Thomas Pynchon* (1974), which is available only in the dustiest alcove of some used bookstores. (I found mine at a potpourri junk and antique store in Lindsborg, Kansas.) The Slade book is part of the series *Writers for the 70s*, which includes analyses of Kurt Vonnegut, Richard Brautigan, Hermann Hesse, J.R.R. Tolkien, and Carlos Castaneda.* Slade gives a potential Pynchon reader some background in history, references to other literary works, examples of Pynchon's zaniness, and insights into his preoccupation with paranoia.

---

* Hardly a pantheon of literary greats, but isn't it interesting to see which writers get lumped together?

As of this writing, I've started on Pynchon's *Against the Day* (2006), a book of biblical proportions that requires slow, meditative reading. So far I like it quite a bit, because I think the novel, which begins with the 1893 World's Columbian Exposition in Chicago—an event that was a coming out party for capitalism—is a metaphor for the common man's struggle against the dark powers of capitalism. In the early going, several of the characters are anarchists (non-joiners) who like to use dynamite ("nitro, the medium of truth," writes Pynchon) to strike back against their oppressors. It's smart thinking by Pynchon. Instead of trying to lasso the current times, which are constantly changing, he steps back a century to an era that he can get his arms around. Pynchon seems to be making the same point that the creator-writer-producer David Simon makes in the HBO series *The Wire*—that capitalism isn't a social policy. Again, I continue to toy around with the idea of providing this helpful information to others, since I am dying to yak about it ad nauseam in the guise of a book group leader, but I fear starting such a group would make me a kind of oppressor, forcing my views and opinions on others.

For the longest time this Pynchon book club fantasy remained a comfortable daydream. Then a year or two ago, a bookstore in Knoxville offered space for a Marcel Proust reading group, moderated by a professor from nearby Maryville College. I debated right up to the time of the second meeting (I missed

the first) whether to go or not. I had been assigned
Proust (like Faulkner) in college, and later on read
the first two volumes of *In Search of Lost Time* on my
own, with a little help from Roger Shattuck's *Marcel
Proust* (1974).*

As you might expect, the energetic woman leading the Proust group was a little eccentric. She wore
antique-style dresses with big floppy hats and could
roll those French words off her tongue without the
slightest hesitation (as opposed to someone like me,
who gets tired of saying "Excuse my French"). Her
knowledge of French literature was impressive if
not out of control. (She wanted to start up an Hon-
oré de Balzac group, too.) Even more helpful were
the two veteran readers who had previously read
the book. At first, I feared they would lord it over
us with *À la recherche du temps perdu* merit badges,
but they ended up providing us with another layer
of understanding, and more importantly, with the
encouragement to keep reading, assuring us that
it was worth the effort. Another participant was so
madly in love with Proust that she would literally
tear up at some passages. It took several months
before I became comfortable with the dozen or
so Prousters. (There was even talk about taking a
trip to France together, but I wasn't *that* comfortable with them.) What I liked about the group was

---

* *In Search of Lost Time* used to be translated as *Remembrance of
Things Past*.

that it provided, in a small city dominated by college football and mega-churches, a little haven for Knoxville eccentrics, which I suppose included myself. Such non-mainstream people are not easy to find.

From reading the first three volumes of *In Search of Lost Time* with this group (a hundred pages per month), I have dozens of index cards of quotes and notes, which I can still pick up randomly to revisit some of my favorite passages. I'm not going to begin to try to explain Proust or what it means to read him or how he wrote about society or the role art (music, theater, and literature) can play in life or that our memories are like eddies in a stream constantly shifting in flow and intensity.*

In addition to learning exponentially more about Proust, what was illuminating for me—a non-joiner —was that a book group works best when it focuses in depth on a particular masterwork. You know what you are signing up for—I mean, you don't go to a book group that focuses on Jane Austen and say, "I want to read Patricia Cornwell." More important, you are able to bond with other readers, which is unusual, because reading is a solitary activity, and you're motivated to keep reading during those long

* The most succinct explanation comes from the Monty Python sketch, the "All-England Summarize Proust Competition," where contestants have fifteen seconds to summarize *In Search of Lost Time* in both swimsuit and evening wear.

stretches of dry, impenetrable prose that are characteristic of a classic. (Remember, Mark Twain defined a classic as a book that everyone talks about but nobody reads.) Proust and Pynchon are no different. Sometimes they can be so obsessed with the most meaningless scene (in the case of Proust) or the most nonsensical interlude (in the case of Pynchon) that you just want to scream. That's why you need the group, to share your pain and motivate you to press on to find those next fascinating nuances and threads. It's too much for one person, really.

Of course, if you're in this kind of reading group you sound "stuck-up" or like someone who puts on airs, which is in direct conflict with my Midwestern heritage.* It's not that I am ashamed that I read these books, but I don't want people to get the false impression that I am some literary expert. I've put in time with Proust, Pynchon, Charles Dickens, Albert Camus, and Fyodor Dostoevsky, but I am ignorant of the Greeks, the Brontës, Jane Austen, and Leo Tolstoy, and thus could easily be exposed as a fraud (just like if you ask me questions about wine and cheese). I'm not even comfortable if you quiz me about Pynchon or Proust, because I do not understand them well enough to explain them, but I do understand them well enough to appreciate the breadth of their intellect and imagination. It's like understanding the different levels of a great film such as *Citizen Kane*, or

* Anyone who reads Proust gets the same reaction as the funny but suicidal scholar played by Steve Carell in the movie *Little Miss Sunshine*.

the music of Charlie Parker.* Another benefit of such a book group is that once you've plowed through a classic you have license to borrow or recite from the work guilt-free.

That's one of the major advantages of reading someone like Proust, Pynchon, or whoever your favorite classic writer may be. These writers cover universal themes and experiences that have contemporary usefulness. For instance, if you bite into a French crème cake and it reminds you of a French crème cake your mother used to make and it brings back a flood of memories, you are allowed to say how the French crème is reminiscent of madeleine soaked in lime-blossom tea in Proust's *In Search of Lost Time*, and you know to say *In Search of Lost Time* instead of *Remembrance of Things Past*, and anyone who says *Remembrance of Things Past* doesn't know squat, and you can call them out on it or you can just go back to writing long, long sentences like you-know-who.

If Pynchon is your man, you are allowed to appropriate any of the five proverbs for paranoids in *Gravity's Rainbow* such as "*You* hide, they seek," and my favorite and the most useful proverb, number 3: "If they can get you asking the wrong questions, they

* Coincidentally, Pynchon gives Charlie Parker his due early in the novel *V.* (1964): "He [Parker] was the greatest alto on the postwar scene and when he left it some curious negative will—a reluctance and refusal to believe in the final, cold fact—possessed the lunatic fringe to scrawl in every subway station, on sidewalks, in pissoirs, the denial: Bird Lives."

Searching for Thomas Pynchon

After I graduated from college, my cousin and I rented a six-room, fifth-story apartment overlooking the grain-elevator- and dying-factory-town-skyline of Danville, Illinois, a small city that never really recovered from the recession of the mid-1970s. Adjacent to the pockmarked downtown of thrift stores and palm readers, this old apartment house was inhabited mostly by paranoid senior citizens, who understandably remained suspicious of us until they realized that we were just easy-going, respectable young adults not unlike their favorite can-do-no-wrong grandsons.

One of the few non-seniors who lived on our floor was a man, fortyish, with a high-brainy forehead and horn-rimmed glasses, who kept to himself except that he was a compulsive walker. He played lots of classical music on his hi-fi stereo. You could see his bust of Beethoven or hear a violin sonata every time he opened his apartment door. When he wasn't in his room, he could be found walking rapidly around the downtown mall, muttering to himself and feverishly smoking his pipe. My cousin and I had a standing joke that this guy was Thomas Pynchon, who you may know is a determined recluse *à la* J. D. Salinger, refusing to be photographed or interviewed. Danville was then and is now a perfect place to hide out. There was nothing stimulating in this small city to distract a dedicated writer.

One day the building maintenance man, a retired black man named Dix with a clean-shaven dome, asked me, since I had a lot of books in my apartment, whether I wanted some more. I knew Dix had visited my place a number of times, since he left the lingering odor of his unlit, partially smoked cigar as a business card every time he unclogged my sink or fixed my radiator. He took me down to the basement where "Pynchon's" possessions were piled on the floor. Dix told me that the strange man had moved, leaving a note bequeathing all his belongings to Dix. There were stacks of books, along with a stereo, records, and a television. Right off, Dix reminded me that the TV and stereo were his, but the rest of the stuff was mine and I could name my price. I bought some framed art reprints, including Rembrandt's *Man in a Golden Helmet*, some classical records, music reference books, and the entire eleven-volume set of Will and Ariel Durant's *The Story of Civilization* for about ten dollars. Given Pynchon's encyclopedic knowledge of history, the book collection reinforced my illusion/joke that this was actually the secretive author's temporary library.

I felt a bit funny about paying so little for a great set of books, but Dix said he was probably just going to haul them to the landfill if I didn't take them. I didn't think to ask Dix whether one of the senior residents might be interested in the collection, but Dix being a practical fellow probably viewed such a course of action as merely postponing the problem instead of being rid of the books once and for all.

don't have to worry about answers." By reading any of Pynchon's books (usually *The Crying of Lot 49* is considered the best one to start with because it is short), you are permitted to use the word "Pynchon-esque" to describe hard-to-read, paranoid-laced novels with dashes of technology, science, and history and two-dimensional characters.*

If there is a negative to joining a book group in order to read one book or author, it's that eventually that vein gets tapped out, and then the group is left with the choice of disbanding or finding a new book or author—which reintroduces the agony of picking a book for someone else or having someone pick a book for you. It's a delicate decision, but if you can get with a group that picks books that you like reading together, like my lifelong friend from Kansas who has been with the same book group for twenty years (not the same books, wine, and cheese group), then you have found something special.

In the meantime, while I look for a group or debate whether to start my own Pynchon group (I'm not ready to do the online thing yet), I'll continue to pick up bargain copies of *Gravity's Rainbow* and

---

* Another way to introduce yourself to a more readable Pynchon is to start with some of his nonfiction pieces. One is a review of Gabriel García Márquez's *Love in the Time of Cholera* (1988); another is the essay "Is it Okay to Be a Luddite?" Or you might pick up a heavily discounted copy of his book of early short stories, *Slow Learner* (1984). The stories themselves are not much, but the essay in which Pynchon describes himself as a young writer is wonderfully clear and entertaining.

Against the Day. I'm even thinking about doing some synopsis notes for *Against the Day* (not to be confused with laborious annotations, which are available on the web), just to help keep the story straight in my own head and so possibly help others as well.* A book group can be a wonderful thing, but it has to be done right.

---

* In the Random House (1981) and Penguin (2004) editions of Proust, each volume contains a brief synopsis in the back, which is immeasurably valuable when reading him.

CHAPTER 14

Managing the Personal Library

Part 1: Storage Shelves of the Soul

When a longtime friend once came to visit me, his initial reaction to my home décor was "Where are all the books? I thought you'd have more books." Upon further review he noted that I did have *some* books, scattered throughout my apartment instead of being assigned to a central location like a study. Had he looked further, he also would have noticed that I forgo organization, eschewing all systems equally, whether they be the Dewey Decimal classification (favored by public libraries), the Library of Congress classification (favored by colleges and universities), or the more "natural" Light-Through-a-Prism schema that organizes the books by the color of their covers (favored by decorators). Currently my personal book collection is a series of branch libraries serving the various constituencies of my own interests. The breakdown goes something like this:

- Living room—antique glass-fronted bookcase from my grandmother. Since this bookcase is in a high traffic area, I use it as a showcase for the more impressive literature: the Proust, the Camus, the ill-gotten Durant *Story of Civilization*, and the personally priceless first edition of Robert Alter's *Heroes in Blue and Gray*. I also keep a few eclectic titles here, the Henry Millers, the Bukowskis, and the Célines, just to keep any voyeurs off-balance.

- Main hallway—a small antique oak bookcase. This area is dedicated to the works of writers I've known or met. These include two travel books by Kim Trevathan and a fine book of short stories set in Louisiana by one of Kim's friends, Tim Parrish, titled *Red Stick Men* (2000). The Parrish book is a sentimental favorite, since a blurb of my favorable review was reprinted in the paperback edition (only time that ever happened). Also housed in this small unit are the works of Madison Smartt Bell and book shopper Dave's wife, Laurie Blauner. I keep two short story collections here by Patricia Henley, from whom I took a couple of writing courses at Purdue University. (I doubt she would remember me for my writing, but she may recall the student who chose *Tropic of Capricorn* for a class reading.) There are copies of my own essays from *Elysian Fields Quarterly*, a baseball literary magazine that I have contributed to regularly over the years. And there are extra copies of my first book, *Understanding Search Engines*, which I co-authored with Michael W. Berry, a few of which are still hermetically sealed for quick resale.* A debate continues on whether to put my ex-mother-in-law's cookbook on that bookcase. Or is that inviting bad karma?

- Study—three bookcases, none of which belong to me (though the books do).† There's a tall folding bookcase for technical reference books about computers and software programs (mostly untouched) and several information-visualization books, which is another interest of mine. A second bookcase holds books about reading or reference guides to contemporary authors that I use as ready reference for my work on *The Book Shopper.*‡ A third homemade bookcase is tucked in the corner. It serves as a holding area for new arrivals or books I'm not sure I'm going to read or don't know exactly what I'm going to do with.
- Bedroom—two bookcases. I have one small, sturdy, deep-shelved tank of a bookcase earmarked for baseball books, which are published in various shapes, sizes, and weights (think encyclopedia). The other bookcase in my bedroom is a flimsy pine structure, which I picked up at a used bookstore's going-out-of business sale. (I guess profiting from

---

* That's not to say the book was a dud. It's been in print for ten years, and we've sold over 4,000 copies, a statistic that Mike and I are both proud of. It's just the kind of book that you can't hand out to all your friends.

† For the record, all three bookcases in the study belong to my older daughter, Cynthia. I am magnanimously keeping them for her until she becomes more permanently settled. She doesn't mind, since when she visits she sleeps in the extra bed located in the study, finding comfort snoozing next to a few of her own possessions.

‡ "Ready reference" is a term that librarians use for the handiest books kept within reach of the reference desk.

the misfortunes of others is the key to building a good library.) The pine bookcase has most of my main book shopper authors (Hijuelos, Harrison, Proulx), and since the books are mostly fiction, I do alphabetize them. On the bottom shelf I keep my favorite humor books.

Relatively speaking, though, I have plenty of books. The size of my collection may not meet the expectations of others because I adhere to one of the adages from library school: "A weeded collection is a used collection." This refers to the library practice of removing unwanted, dated, or unread books so patrons can more readily locate the books they really want. The library's logic goes something like this: If the books people want cannot be found easily, people are less inclined to visit the library. Not only does weeding benefit the library's browsing users, but it serves as a main supply source for those annual Friends of the Library book sales.

Weeding also is critical for someone like me who moves at regular intervals. I always use a move as an opportunity to reassess my collection. Before my last relocation, from Knoxville to Atlanta, I sold about ten boxes of books to a couple of local book dealers and returned home having purchased only one box—a net loss of nine boxes. As one might expect, I used my store credit to pick up a few new (albeit used) books and to replace a worn paperback or two with hardbacks.

Despite efforts to keep my library under control, I still have managed to achieve some notoriety among people in the moving trade. One time when I was making a local move, I hired the guy who had done a previous move for me that had required hauling a piano down two flights of stairs. Now, I've worked out at a number of gyms in my life, but I have never seen a feat of strength like this. This man with a muscular V-shaped torso held the lower end of the piano while his two assistants balanced the upper end as they moved slowly down the stairs. A few years later, when I went to hire him again, the man complained, "I remember you—all the books! Do you still have all those books?" To him, moving pianos, sleeper sofas, and refrigerators was biz as usual, but moving several dozen boxes of books was an inexplicable frivolity. After all, you can only read one book at a time. I tried to explain that, compared to others, I was a lightweight in this department. For instance, when book shopper Dave relocated from Boston to Seattle back in the 1980s, he shipped an estimated 150 boxes of books, a load that his mover described as "the heaviest non-commercial move" he had ever done.

Even though it is inconvenient to move books, bibliophiles often find Sophie's-choicing through their collection unimaginable. Many worry that they would be getting rid of books they might want back. This is a legitimate concern—especially if it is the last copy on Earth. I can personally relate to this fear, since I recall repurchasing certain books that I had purged. Mary Karr's *Liars' Club* and Carolyn Chute's *The Beans of Egypt, Maine* come readily to mind. On the other hand, I have probably disposed of hundreds of books, so what is that—a two or three percent regret rate? Not bad. Moreover, keeping the collection under control alleviates the more frustrating problem of not being able to find a book in my library without a lot of head scratching and tearing through unmarked boxes of books.

There's another reason to keep that personal library properly maintained. Book collections are like little windows into a reader's soul, are they not? Aren't we what we have read (or think we might want to read)? I know that when I am in someone else's house, I check out what they are reading.* And because I expect the same treatment when I have a visitor at my house, I carefully display selected literature to keep my voyeurs guessing and engaged. The perusal of my bookshelves is a quick way to get to know me.

Of course we will all reach a point when we must leave our possessions, even books, behind. This is a delicate subject and one worthy of its own chapter. But first, a related anecdote . . .

---

* I'm especially unabashed about looking at people's books during home tours in exclusive neighborhoods. You usually see three types of book collections on display: 1) A large library with lots of crappy bestsellers. 2) A modest library resembling "what every good used bookstore should have." 3) Picture or arty books strategically placed as props or pedestals for vases and other decorative objects.

Fahrenheit 451

Ironically, part of my passion for reading developed from watching a movie—on TV, no less. The movie was *Fahrenheit 451*, an adaptation of the novel by science-fiction writer Ray Bradbury. I must have been about twelve or thirteen years old at the time.

Fahrenheit 451 (not to be confused with *Fahrenheit 9/11*, the Michael Moore documentary) is set in a dystopian future where a totalitarian government tries to eliminate all books and other printed material from society. To enforce these strict laws, a security force of "firemen" set fire to books. (Book paper burns at 451 degrees Fahrenheit.) By controlling information, they hope to control the populace. Besides, as one of the fireman leaders says (and I'm paraphrasing), "Books contradict each other. One writer says one thing; another writer says something entirely different. Books make people unhappy."

When I watched this movie, I didn't realize that *Fahrenheit 451* had a fancy pedigree: It was directed by the famous François Truffaut and stars Oskar Werner, a talented actor and stage director, and Julie Christie (who shared a bungalow in the Russian steppes with Omar Sharif in *Dr. Zhivago*), with music by Bernard Herrmann of *Psycho* fame. Werner plays the rebellious Montag, who develops a love of books along with a relationship with a member of the book-reading underground played by Christie in a Twiggy haircut. Finally Werner gets tired of watching his wife (also played by Christie) watch TV and joins the underground, whose members memorize books and "become them" until the times change.

Years later, as an experiment to test the lingering power of *Fahrenheit 451*, I decided to rent the movie for my thirteen-year-old daughter's sleepover. I knew Cynthia's school chums were readers, and though the future portrayed in the movie "looked kind of old," they sat through the whole thing and were collectively outraged when stacks of books were torched. (I wondered if they used real books or book stand-ins.) At the end of the movie my daughter vowed to keep all her Christopher "Hack-up-the-Babysitter" Pike books and save them for posterity. The movie ended up having a more far-reaching effect than I initially intended, since I have towed some of my daughter's books around with me as well.

Part 2: The Final Weeding

The short Bookmark about *Fahrenheit 451* serves as a bridge between the storage and space issues covered in part 1 of this chapter and the meatier dilemmas presented here in part 2. At the risk of embarrassing Cynthia, I like to bring out the anecdote about saving her Christopher Pike* books because after view-

---

* Christopher Pike is the pseudonym (borrowed from a *Star Trek* episode) of the author Kevin McFadden.

ing *Fahrenheit 451* and seeing books burned (one character decides to burn with her books, which included—of all things—a *Mad* magazine paperback), she had the same response that I did at my first viewing of the movie. I was in my thirties before I could loosen my grip on every book I had ever bought. Now in her mid-twenties, Cynthia is still holding on to nearly all of her books, but as she begins to change residences more often, I am noticing this predilection start to ebb.

As you would expect, I have enabled her behavior. Even more frightening, Cynthia recognizes my weakness and—as all smart children do—works it to her advantage. How could I refuse to store her books, or complain when she asks me to ship boxes of them to her at regular intervals? She knows I won't call in a *Fahrenheit 451* fireman to remedy the problem. She knows that I totally approve of reading and the value of reading. Of course, the true test of love and book storage comes when you die and somebody has to dispose of your library.

Those of us who have not moved on "from the foreplay of life to the terror of the unknown" can only speculate about what we will be allowed to take with us.* We could request that a few of our favorite books be placed in the casket, not unlike the custom of woodland tribes who buried hunting

* This quote comes from David Johansen, host of the metaphysical radio program *Mansion of Fun.*

knives, arrowheads, and fish hooks with their dead for use in the hereafter. Of course, if one chooses to be cremated, this is not an option. At best, we may be able to take books with us in the form of favorite passages or ideas that have become woven into the fabric of our consciousness. Little snippets such as "Nature does not know extinction; all it knows is transformation" (opening epigraph from Pynchon's *Gravity's Rainbow* [1973]) may go with us into the ether.

For those left behind—well, it's a waste of energy to try to dictate to your children the books they should salvage or whether they should just put in a call to the local fireman. Trying to rule from the grave will only lead to discord. However, I cannot resist offering some guidance to my daughters before I go to make their decisions easier. My advice can be summed up in the simple directive, "Remember, girls, you are book shoppers, goddamn it, and you shouldn't pass up the chance to pick up some quality books for free."

I admit that this advice is hypocritical, since I myself retained only a few books from my own paternal grandmother and my father. My grandmother was a big believer in libraries, so she didn't keep a lot of books in the house to begin with. When she died, I cleaned out her antique bookcase and hauled half a dozen boxes of books to my place in West Lafayette to go through at my leisure. I even invited my book shopper neighbor (see the Bookmark "Book Neighbor" at the end of this chapter) to help me look over her collection.

Upon my father's death, I kept several boxes of his Ballantine's *Illustrated History of World War II* series for nearly two decades before deciding to find a home for them at a reputable used bookstore in Knoxville. Later I discovered that many of these books were worth something monetarily since they are long out of print and have become popular with World War II history buffs. Rather than suffering seller's remorse, I am comforted to know that the books are again in the hands of those who value them as my father did.

I did keep a few of my father's personal favorites, most notably two books about World War I. One is a yellowed paperback of Guy Chapman's *A Passionate Prodigality*, an autobiographical account written in 1933. The other is Alistair Horne's *The Price of Glory* (1962), a book about the Battle of Verdun.* Knowing that he liked this type of book, I am momentarily saddened that my father wasn't around to read Pat Barker's *Regeneration* trilogy. I've placed the Chapman and Horne books on the homemade bookshelf in the study that is reserved for books to be read.

---

* Upon further investigation, I discovered Horne remains a relevant writer. His book *A Savage War of Peace: Algeria 1954–1962*, originally published in 1977, was reprinted in 2006 because historians and policymakers saw stark parallels between the French in Algeria and the United States in Iraq. I recall my father poring over Horne's Verdun book.

Deciding what books to keep from a loved one's library can be a personal tribute to the departed as well as to the books. It can be an exercise loaded with gut-wrenching emotion or desolate bleakness, but it doesn't have to be. In my view, the best way to tackle this task is to wait until your emotions settle, even if takes a couple of years. It's not like the books are going to "spoil," unless, of course, you put them in a wet basement or garage.

Later—probably when you have to move—you will again have the opportunity to assess the collection. A few books will resurface emotionally, and those are the ones to keep. Try to find a decent home for the others and don't worry about it. You've spent sufficient time and thought on this project, and that's homage enough.

Even my own book collection, which I've kept to a manageable number of volumes (in my eyes, at least), is not above a final assessment. Better to put most of the books back in circulation than store them in boxes waiting to be cursed by some stevedore who loathes the printed word. Put the few books that survive this most vigorous weeding prominently on display, preferably in that antique glass-fronted bookcase that holds the best your library has to offer.

Book Neighbor

Because of their proximity to Purdue University, West Lafayette, Indiana, neighborhoods in the late 1980s were usually filled with either run-down student rentals or stylish professorial homes. There were also a few areas in between, like our own subdivision. Our neighborhood was part of the post-WWII, middle-class manufactured-housing boom. Lower level Purdue staffers and married grad students with families inhabited these ranch-style, particleboard houses slapped onto concrete slabs.

My neighbor Ed, who looked like a middle-aged version of Beetlejuice, worked at one of the libraries at Purdue while his wife, Grace, stayed at home. And stay at home she did, because she didn't drive. If she needed to go somewhere like the grocery store, either Ed or their teenaged son might drive her, but she preferred to walk or take the bus. They had a daughter who lived nearby and was producing a child at the rate of one every two years, and Grace often took care of them. She was a tall, religious woman with small eyes that seemed to be blinded by any direct light. Grace often sighed when she talked—the embodiment of Christian suffering.

Like most houses on the block, theirs didn't have a garage, and the yard was cluttered with children's toys, yard equipment, and a few auto parts. Their heavy-set teenaged son used the parts to customize noisy, smelly Detroit steel gas hogs into louder, noisier pieces of junk. The grass usually went uncut, but this was by design. Grace was in the process of converting both front and back yards into green zones, complete with groundcover, flowers, vegetables, and herbs. It was a process that was taking years.

Ed was more interested in book collecting. Every Saturday morning, he and Grace would set out in their Marathon automobile (a converted Checker Cab) on a milk-run of garage and estate sales to scavenge books for themselves and toys for their grandchildren. With extra room in the back seat, not to mention a large trunk and heavy suspension system, the Marathon could haul plenty.

This went on for years, and I wondered where they put all their purchases. Sometimes when picking up my daughter from playing with their granddaughter, I'd catch a glimpse inside and see that the place was filling up. One day, when Ed came over to look at some books I had rescued from my grandmother's estate, he invited me to see his library—something I had always wanted to do.

Several steps inside confirmed that Ed's house, like the yard, had been allowed to return to its natural state, but downstairs in the basement (a rarity in our neighborhood) it was a different story. Ed had built rows of shelves from floor to ceiling and filled them with books (he specialized in books about bookmaking and engineering). In the center of the room were a lamp and a worn recliner where he obviously spent much of his time reading. The room was climate controlled, in contrast to the rest of the house. It was Ed's personal sanctuary, where he could relax and read surrounded by his book-hunting bounty.

The trait about Ed and Grace (and she was a book person, too, in her own way—constantly walking the grandchildren to the library) I most admired was that despite the disarray on the outside of their lives, with their restless children and active grandchildren always buzzing around, they never seemed upset about how things were going. I figure it was the calming effect of the books.

CHAPTER 15

Parting Words

*What is most appealing about young folks, after all,
is the changes, not the still photograph of finished
character but the movie, the soul in flux. Maybe this
small attachment to my past is only another case of
what Frank Zappa calls a bunch of old guys sitting
around playing rock 'n' roll. But as we all know, rock
'n' roll will never die, and education too, as Henry
Adams always sez, keeps going on forever.*
—Thomas Pynchon, Introduction to *Slow Learner*

EVERYONE HAS HEARD STORIES about the difficul-
ties encountered by authors seeking to publish a
book, and my story is no different. *The Book Shopper* has endured the standard mountain of rejec-
tions from agents and publishers alike, and has been
rewritten twice. I wouldn't say that I had given up
hope, but I will admit that the occasional handwritten note of encouragement from an editorial assistant
was providing less and less sustenance. Fortunately,
through the serendipity of book shopping, I finally
connected with a publisher for this book.

201

I was living in Knoxville at the time and driving to Atlanta every other weekend to be with my friend Denise and look for a new job (in that order). One weekend we found our way to a small, surprisingly eclectic museum bookstore on the campus of Emory University. While browsing, I picked up Gabriel Zaid's *So Many Books: Reading and Publishing in an Age of Abundance* (2003) and noted it was published by Paul Dry Books of Philadelphia, a press I was not familiar with. I purchased and read this tidy little collection of thirteen essays, and realized that this was an author—and by extension a publisher—who thought about the book life the way I did. This gem of a shop exceeded my definition of a good bookstore, which is, as you already know by now, measured in the degree that I feel a tug on my wallet—and a willingness even to pay full price, as I did that day for the Zaid book. It is possible that if I hadn't gone browsing in that store on that day (and I did scour the remainder table first), *The Book Shopper* would never have been published.

Looking back, I really shouldn't be surprised that I stumbled upon a publisher while I was book shopping. For me, book shopping and connecting with the community of readers in odd sorts of ways have always been enriching experiences, and I don't just mean in a monetary way. Book shopping has been a personal guerrilla action against the "mass culture, mass superstition [and] mass slogans" that characterize our modern times, as Alfred Kazin wrote in

his introduction to John Dos Passos's U.S.A. trilogy.*
I know I am not alone in my desire for less technology and entertainment. As David Shi points out
in *The Simple Life: Plain Living and High Thinking in
American Culture* (1985), from colonial times a percentage of the populace has made an effort to slow
down the pace of life and embrace its meaningful
aspects. Keeping one's life simple in terms of possessions (and activities) frees up time and energy for
reading, thinking, and writing. I really like that Shi
is neither sentimental nor dictatorial about trying
to translate simplicity into a way of living, and he
makes a distinction between choosing to live without possessions and security, and just being poor.†
The Book Shopper tries to tap into this philosophy in
the belief that applying a touch of the brakes to our
fast-paced lives will enrich them.

Besides showing you the enrichment of my life
that comes from reading good books, I have also
tried to express an appreciation for the camaraderie among readers, a source of great satisfaction and
friendship. The people mentioned throughout these

---

* The three books of the Dos Passos trilogy are *The 42nd Parallel*
(1930), *1919* (1932), and *The Big Money* (1936), which all focus on
life in America in the first quarter of the twentieth century—before
the United States became a global superpower.

† This distinction is important. People in Shi's *Simple Life* are not
those who constantly struggle to pay food bills, housing bills, or
medical bills. It's one thing to volunteer for simplicity, another for
it to be mandated.

pages have added as much character to my own life-manuscript as they have to this book. The thought that such people may no longer exist in the digital future is one I refuse to buy into. Even in a worst-case scenario, there will *still* be book people. The future may be like that final sequence in Truffaut's *Fahrenheit 451*, when Montag flees into the countryside and joins a renegade book club where each member must memorize a book to gain admittance. Everyone there lives peaceably, and all are committed to keeping The Word alive until the time that books are reintroduced into society. I just haven't figured out whether, if that time comes, I should memorize something significant like *Gravity's Rainbow* or something I pretty much know by heart already such as *Heroes in Blue and Gray.*

But until that time, I take comfort in knowing that in a world fraught with conformity, where you see the same retail stores, smell the same fast foods, and hear the same music on the car radio no matter where you are, there still exists a tribe of nonconformists. These people (including you, dear reader) are like that beloved used bookstore near a campus town with inventory piled high and deep. Only you know where certain books (the ones with your favorite ideas, quotes, and snippets of description that capture your life experience) can be found. Through years of reading, an individual becomes one of those places that I never want to give up visiting. In a world that seemingly wants to pave us over, reading remains a refuge—and the backwater neighborhood where I, at least, will always choose to live. Thanks for taking the time to stop by and listen to my stories. Please, do come again.

Acknowledgments for Troublemakers

WHAT MAKES *TROUBLEMAKERS*, a collection of short stories by John McNally published in 2000, memorable extends beyond the bleak portrayal of what it's like to grow up in the Midwest. What I remember most is McNally's acknowledgment to his troublemaker friends—the thugs, the riffraff, and the tireless readers who helped him write the book.

We all have troublemaker friends and colleagues who help with our books. And I'd like to say thank you to the people who took the trouble to inspire, read rough drafts, edit, and provide encouragement either directly or indirectly during the ten plus years it took to prepare this manuscript.

First and foremost is Denise Casey, a tough editor, who over the years has helped to refine my voice and keep my writing on task without disturbing the personality and vision of this book. Denise is my best friend, with whom I share my morning coffee and my random thoughts—a person who appreciates my uncombed state of mind. This book simply would never have been completed without her editing, friendship, and love.

Other people have been important in this book shopper's life, too. In the early stages of certain chapters I bounced ideas off my daughter Cynthia and my good friend Bill Gwin, who is a useful combination of English teacher and librarian in Oak Ridge, Tennessee. Then there is my other daughter, Bonnie, whose energy and outrageousness have provided little blurbs of originality that have been spun into paragraphs and parts of chapters. I know that my daughters are proud of me for finishing this, and they have offered encouragement every step of the way.

I would be a lousy son and author if I didn't acknowledge that my mother, Jean Browne, was the person who read a lot to me as a child and has always been supportive of me. I'd also like to recognize the memories of my father, Glenn, and my late sister, Kay. One of my best memories of Kay is of her sitting on my patio, smoking a cigarette, drinking a Diet Mountain Dew, and cranking through my entire manuscript (circa 2003) in a few hours. Then there is my brother, Neil, who reinforced the premise that the rawness of our Midwestern youth played some role in how we knew the world.

To Kim Trevathan, a fellow Cubs fan and a teacher at Maryville College, who helped in the early versions of the book, I say thanks. Of course, you already know about Dave Dintenfass and Laurie Blauner of Seattle, who have their own chapter. My appreciation also goes out to Tom Nelson, a Midwesterner of few words—so when he says something nice you know it really means something—and longtime friend Ian Joyce, who provided encouragement and expertise in developing this book's online presence (www.thebookshopper.org). Thanks to Dr. Bill Robinson, a now retired professor from the School of Information Sciences at the University of Tennessee, who shouldn't be held responsible if my opinions about librarianship are misdirected. To my friends Bruce Woods of Wichita (who is a member of Kansas's most renowned book group) and John Stuhl of Knoxville I also extend my appreciation for their guidance along the way. And finally, thanks to publisher Paul Dry. He recognized a rough manuscript of strange ideas and cared enough to make it something worth "sending out into the world."

Index of Authors and Titles